Cassiopeia

Lying EASTWARD

Original poems on love & life
in the heart of the
English countryside

Mark Whelehan

CASSIOPEIA LYING EASTWARD
Original poems on love & life in the
heart of the English countryside
Copyright © 2017 by Mark Whelehan (author)
Cover illustration by Will Mirehouse

First published in Great Britain in 2017 by
Ditty Box Publishing
(a division of Ditty Box Ltd. Reg. No. 4602831)

A CIP catalogue record for this book is available from the
British Library

First Edition
CASSIOPEIA LYING EASTWARD
Mark Whelehan

ISBN: 978-0-9564899-5-1

These verses, for what they are worth, are
sculpted words from a man revelling in nature.
He finds a bucolic setting with a
stream running through it.
He discovers a peace and equilibrium
and experiences a rare love with someone;
something he believed was beyond him.
He finds there a paradise on earth
which inspires the art in him.

Dedicated to:

Family and friends
here, there & everywhere...
for putting me up, and
putting up with me!

Contents

Cassiopeia Lying Eastward

As light crept in the fading July starlit sky
A familiar double you threw a last wink
North across her shoulder to the Great bear
… Cassiopeia lying eastward in the rising sun
Dying waved goodbye…

Your hair like sunshine shook
And shards sparkled as they fell
In Crookwood Brook
Though cloudy from the rains
Hit the surface and bounced back again

Your peel of laughter rang
As it echoed through the tunnel
Neath the road rebounding
Echoes still on the cold brick sides
Of that half leat that churns up leaves
And slides
Like memories from the past
That caused the bridge once a ford
Where your ice green eyes
Fluttered as they focused toward me

God the ephemeral spray that hit our faces
Woke us up and made us gasp now gone
Now when I pause to hone my scythe
I hear it in the rasp
And in the high up buzzard cry
I hear you shouting back
Your last goodbye
I never counted how many days without
You became the past
I only know that with you time flew
But at the same time
Forever did it last

The Wiltshire Woodquest and the Dove

Summer

Shadowy twilight covers the downs,
Shading my garden greenery,
Slowly spreading and deep'ning the gloom,
Darkens the still and soundless air,

And then

"My toe bleeds Betty, My toe bleeds,
Betty, my toe bleeds Betty, Look!"
And so on calling and calling,
With infinite repetition,

Later

Calls from a nearby clump of trees,
Cousin rock dove mutters advice,
"Cure it, Cure it, Cure it, Cure it,"
An alternating duet 'til,

Nightfall.

Seos Whelehan

The Lawns at Stradbrook Hall

Black patrols of starlings quarter the sun-loved lawns,
Bayonet beaks stabbing the grass relentlessly.
Noisily aloof in their world of taller trees,
Gossipy rooks squabble and fuss among their nests,
A constant, raucous background choir of ceaseless calls.

Under tall copper trees the lawns have darker shades,
Brooding beneath grey boughs, and whisp'ring foliage.
Beyond; the weeping beech spreads its myriad leaves.
Which cloak sprawling, unevenly reclining limbs,
And form leaf-lined caverns, and dim secret caves
Patterned with shimm'ring sunlight and filtered shadows.

Below the curving balcony of tow'ring limes,
A grown-together sea of laurels form a crescent,
That half-circles the granite stairs to make a stage.
Tall sentries of red-hot pokers guard the borders,
And colour the lawn verges leading to these steps,
Where my young brother Peter sits, chin in cupped hands,
Silent; unmoving, save for his slow falling tears,
Staring into the bleak sadness of his future.

Here on the gravel drive his puppy Tan lies dead,
Cruelly broken, and now for once, quiet and still.
He'll have no more morning walks, nor evening ramblings,
Or hear again his requiem traffic at the gate,
That ended his guileless wanderings from the lawns.

Seos Whelehan

Mark Whelehan

Still Time

As the sun sets on our day
Knee deep in buttercups we stray
As that bell tolls the boat has sailed
Still time Still time Still time
And through this vale where time stands still
My poignant memories will haunt me till
I fade away

I have lost love and found it many times
Yet it alludes me now of how
Or why or what it is
And what have I to show for it?
Some say – how sad
Uncle and auntie so and so never wed
But others say that those have less to lose
Whom compromise ain't led.

As the sun slips lower
And drunken cows are lowering their voices
Blurred shadows edge my photograph
A projector flickers in a darkened room
Images we never had

Some say time does not stand still
But it lasted for me forever as I lived
And as that bell tolls
The boat has sailed
Still time Still time Still time.

Hardly Knew Her

I hardly knew her
Still the strains felt were pure
A magnitude of stars
Burst silent as a firework
Displayed itself so splendid in my
Hollow mind
Hallowed, kind I strode resplendent
So bold as to a war
But then so swiftly as it came,
It went
Some light switched off as out of sync
A word or gesture broke the spell
The smell turned sour, I sank
The world rushed sideways, fell,
Away it flew
And nothing new closed in again.

Ducks on a Bare Pond

Lit
Alight
The lighted
Paper burns when
Thrown through a darkened
Room – light-switched on… brightness
Ducks alight on a bare pond

Circling circumnavigating
Ripples converge mirror surface lost
Pure reflections life's blackness and whiteness
Blurred colours festooned abound collide explode
Thought they would rest here but they take flight… a light lit

Burn through the air they flap away to distant water
Look up mouth shaped in 'O' followed by a piece called
Silence!

The Syllabic Hiku Rape

Square fields, yellow patch,
Made you so pissed off, gorgeous.
Bitter waves invade.

Rape, it's guise no quilt.
A bitter rose unfolding,
Shone through shining light.

Smelt like pepper
Sweet-crushed built like a floss, on a
stick, sunk in lemon.

Up climbed a shocking lark,
followed by a peace called
silence, what happened next?

Beyond Me

The bush beyond me,
Becomes even greener as
The light fails.
And in
Faces there hiding,
Sits a bird and sings
Its heart out.

There must be
Something else besides
Sight and sound – I feel it beyond touch.
That thing you get with love – but it's not love.
Whatever it is that bird must be
Getting even more – like a lark that climbs to no ceiling,
Like my dog who runs till he's dead
And then lays on his back in his bed
And whimpers in his sleep
At the hunting in his head.
I watch all these things inadequately.

On Learning I'm in a Hole

I want to say lots of things out loud, on the quiet.
But you know there's little time,
And moaning is so wearisome
When you're in a bigger hole than me.
I'd like to explode like a fragrance,
But it all sound so wet that…
Oh what the hell!
By tomorrow I'll forget, buried in some muse,
While you still sweat and smoke your cigarette
Down to the very bone.

It's all relative they say,
As if it's all relative – it ain't…
It ain't that at all, it's just tough luck.
You look up and say "Hey, it's not that bad, you know."
But it is and I can't say it 'cause it is.
Who gives a shit? No one, but you and I!
You say,
"Don't you look at me like that and don't you fucking cry!"
Yeah! Sure, I won't say a thing.

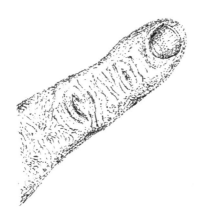

Before During and After a Storm

Why did I not think of that
Slaps hand on head
The beast falls dead, crumples to the floor

A metallic smell
Molten lead, the sky stood still.
Then the torn cloud burst
Its belly, a lark snuffed out,
Fell he from the flash,
A stone. Skimmed the swallow, in
And out the corridor of flies, through listening
Ears of wheat it sailed,
Only as the lull prevailed.

On the soul the colour sin,
In between the sky falls in
All manner of discords began
Trapped inside a smitten tin.
A cell of skin,
A prisoner.
A skin cage.

Dry'za bone once, dust
And ashes sluiced, my dog knee
Deep he labours, gulps,
Savours, stops, looks up to glimpse
The sky roll by, the
Lark climb, crescendos lost in
Azure and a distant
Roll of the drums.

Far Above the Human Bark
(An Old Shilling Spun)

Far above the human bark soar the angels with the lark…
I went out to the cut fields
I couldn't sleep
The smell of early life
New tilth turned chalk mown stalks
All spoke in pungent hues which tasted also
Stunk fresh and stung with heavy dew and dung sweet
So I drank it in
And I traced around some set-aside
And set off to creep
It seemed too early to create a sound so muffled feet
And to see what I could find
And there before I stepped on it a larks nest
With some warm speckled eggs colding
So new   so clean   so bare
'Cept a whisp of feather from la mere.[settled there]

The bird was already rising in the air
Like some farm machinery
Switched on and whirring into life
To start the day so thrilling
So sharp its song cut like an old shilling spun
Like the beginning of a prop-shaft's departure
From its bearing
The early bird climbed
In a vibrating high pitched hum
Became a trilling and put to shame
My accompanying thrum on the bonnet of my strum.

As the millibeats of wing and tongue sailed off
As buffeted and muted by high breezes
This tiny soloist of raging passioned soliloquy

No other sound to focus on
Soared out of sight
The light became so bright
Looking up my sight was stunned
Its voice trailed off in a fashion that rent my heart
Dumbfounded
Because I felt it touch a nerve a chord
Despite these vain attempts
Not explained nor nearly touched upon
By any word!

Where rough men's bark
Was left below while soaring with the lark.
When sat at desk with daily stew
Where minds are heavy with the grind
I hear the drone of some high plane
Which takes and lifts me to another plain
I feel refreshed and better and indeed sane
To have witnessed when out early on a summer's morn
Looking down from long and lofty orisons
Immersed in azure blue
Amongst the angels flying through –
The lark's song.

Host of Angels

Let me fly with you
Below the worn out soles of mice
Parts the cobwebbed morning dew
Where a host of fallen Angels
Bursts through the mental eye of a needle
And into the azure

Hanging by a silken thread
Our souls like drops in purgatory
Now they soar above mankind
These noble selves come care for me
For brief moments all too few
Sweeps their phalanx into view
We flew with Angels and in truth
We landed with them too.

It Is As If the Land is Rolling

It is as if the land is rolling
And the houses on the hill are sliding
Up the crests and down the belly
Down and up careering waves
It takes my eyes and clutched breath with it
But am planted in the pasture
Leant against an old oak tree
Allowing me a balanced outlook
On the rolling country
But still the slate and terracotta
Fashioned by mason and wheels of potter
Moulding slip and clay together
Rooves dip and climb all weathers
On their undulating roundabout
To the thunder of the hooves
Because right by me flies the fox
His eyes and teeth and thoughts are flashing
Leatherclad horses get a thrashin'
Eyes a poppin' cries and screams
And horses dropping
And astrider's blood inflamed
With stirrups cupped and lust are gaining
Riding til you think they'll bust
The scene is shattered for an instance
Then soon gone and in the distance
I look up the land still rolling
With rooves and hooves and hunt improving
And a far off cry of victory.

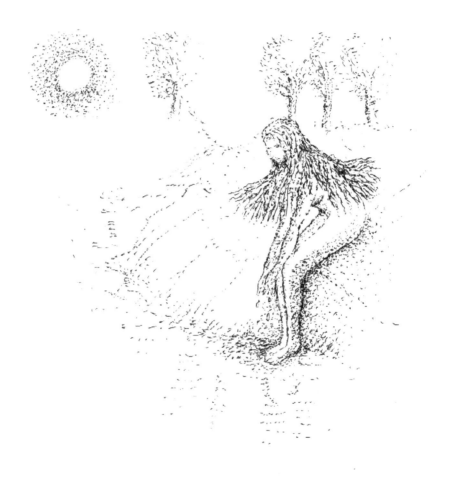

The Otter

I went down beside a stream
Where moons reflection waxed and waned
There was a siren in my head
That was driving me insane

I threw up at the lunar sky an apple
And as it spun I wished that one
Could choose a love that twinkled there beside
That pulled and tore the inner tide
That wrestled mens hearts from their minds

The ripe fruit fell and hit the ground and in that second
In my mind a path was scorched.
And day broke wide across her face
And I transfixed as in a spell

She spoke and I awoke to find
An otter floating down the stream
And on seeing me it dived
A mermaid in another guise

I looked back to the stream a while
And there your image shimmered
And hair-swept tossed about
A silver fish swam in and out

The whole epiphany made me shout
But no sound did come out
Save an owl hoot-distant train
That brought me back to earth again.

I Have a Stream

I have a stream
And in its ripples glow the night
And in its canter read its course to dawn
And the moons face reflects there
And beams a smile
Meanders, threads a thought.

And on its flow I feel braille nipples
As fish rise and in its light are caught
And fight to catch the moon
On reflection my hands work its surface
For some answer.

It is a brook which opens like a book
Its pages washed with ink
Blurred messages plucked discarded
Soon drift and sink
Of loves censure which brought me to the brink

Its edge and bank retreat
Where water meets green sand
Which pours when lifted
Time escaping through my hands

Some say all this dreaming
Never pays
But it is the sum and total of my days
And when I add up all my toil
It is these mental excursions
Which make life tolerable
And who can say this fools foils
Only splash and flounder
When so say sensible people's
High ground subsides
Their happiness is no sounder.

I will bend and dip
And cup my hands and bathe my fevered brow
And catch the moon
And search for ever in its flowing length
That eternal answer to my mental strength

So if you ever see me by my stream
You'll know I am only watching
Nipples break its surface
Soon as fish rise to look through
Watching my face ripple
And glow like the moon

They are no fools these fish
They have seen me smile and laugh and cry and rage
And have watched me growing old
They see my soul
Glow like a dying coal.

Soft as Sleep

Soft as sleep
My mind creeps
Back and back again to see
If those old thoughts long and dusting
Deftly guided out to sea
Waves of consciousness counting
Pulled by lunar solar strings
Feather light and caught in flight
Swim indolent and carefree
All our deeds and machinations
Searching out a sanctuary
Prowl the air and seven oceans
Crossing intermittently.

The Finches

Charm

The day revolves
I muse.
In the oak trees across the field
whisps of teasel tugged and teased
a sprinkling of gold dust tinkling
in warm breezes
coins tossed in the air
sun spangled finches charm
spin untangling rasping lisping wheezing chatter
borne spores of vehement semantics
pour harmless filibustering
unravelling far off strains
wind-drift entrails of fairy bells
faint tintinnabulation rising in hiatus
like muted altar bells of chime
crescendo descends re-rise sing
lilts tilted and flicked
in tiny tongues
lifted off a tiny hymn book
spilling out of a flea circus colosseum.

It's here her soft touch materialises
her gentle constant patient watchful
eyes cast down
as she figures out her maternal chores.
It's in amongst such boisterous minutiae
childlike play her ample duggs feed
I yearn to hold her mother nature close and squeeze
and say it's you who hold the tight reins
the world together on taught lines

stretched cabled rope
concentrated love and hope
which wears you down
in mystic circles and ancient cycles
in unrequited altruistic unconditional
imparted soothing love
and revolutions of time.

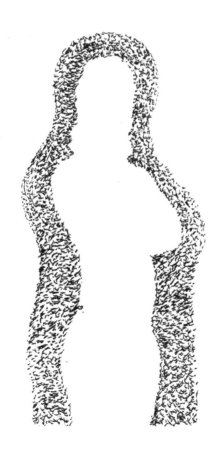

The Sleeping Badger

The sky was sapphire and
Ink-blue flies patterned prettily
On the bare empty wooden table
Scrubbed white
Under where the old apple tree stood
In The Ham Orchard Crookwood.

It was the end of May and midday.
Larking kids echoed in the woods
As the badger deep down in his dry hole
On a newly made bed
Of sweet pungent smelling hay
Rolled on his back luxuriating
And exhaled in abject pleasure.
The cubs were almost ready to leave
And his mate would have much more time
For him once again.

Outside, the cette had been cavorting
Under silver moonlight shadows
In and out the bluebells
Til the magic mists of dawn

As the old grey man yawned
Their yickering spats the only sounds
Save the haunting hoot of tawny owls
And awakening crowing fowls –
When suddenly a
Disturbed woodquest clapped its wings
And they all fled underground.

Now the yellowhammer wheezed its song
"Little bit of bread and nooooooo cheese!"
Goldfinches pitch battled over thistle and teasle.
From the stream
The windblown enigmatic otter's high pitched whistle

A rabbit's scream ambushed by stoat or weasel
And afternoon crept on.
A triumphant horn blew in the far off
And he knew a fox was dead…
These were the things that filled a badger's head.

Blackcap and chiffchaff
Warbled song entwined
Then blew away as sun met moon
Through scented columbine bats flew
The tables fared and donned
As supper at the orchard cracked on.
Clink of glasses as distant church clock chimed
And still he slept

Crept the cattle
Twist of tongue 'rip' and 'chomp'
As overhead the herd
Grazed toward the wood fringe fence
But so slumber held was he
It made no sense.
Neither did he stir
When cloven hooves
Came crashing through the musty lair
Nor heard he the cows groan as they limped away
With broken limbs beyond repair

If he'd looked up
He would have tasted the open air
And been aware, the consequences,
And got his family out of there
But his black and white face
Only seemed to smile wistfully
Ignorance is bliss or so they say
And so he snored and slept
Carefree until another day.

Trapped and Escaping

Early
September
And a lovely
Autumn of my day
An Indian summer came to stay
And as sun set swallows in droves
Flee my way and over me
Indented on the warm bonnet
Of my van-guards
My form

As they twittered
Their mouse like messages
Of communications I lean
And lie against my windscreen
As if I float there suspended in aspic
For seemingly there's nothing at my back [sic]
And if the glass should crack
From how I sit I'd fall
And the gearstick ball
Would force through my neck
A gobstopper to all this.
Still I remain… wittering on

Gazing up at minute specs of life
Unwittingly coincidentally
I gulp the air trapped in my mouth
I almost swallow a midge
Nearly a tiny life wiped out…
Which begs the question of inner strife
How small do you go in respecting life?
They navigated from north south west
Suddenly disappeared in golden bands
And cast a wide vibrating net my mind digests
I fall into a sleep

My grandpa's deep story telling voice
And we spellbound
Eyes wide cross-legged
At his giant slippered feet

Who stole the golden hand?
Who stole the golden hand?
It… was… you!

The accusing finger pointed down at me
I awoke with a start!
And like darts in a liquid air ripple
Out from the molten sun
Two wild ducks scythed through
Les Hirondelles as shot from a gun
Scattered then redirectioning
They negotiated on the wing
Giant banking 'Vs' of geese in rhythmic spells
Crying like orphan calves
Searching for a milky pool to settle on
By evening.

But still I heard them sing
Chiding the frosts at all costs
Was oh! so chastening.
Even when the engorged bull
Marched across the home field
Bellowing his lustful sin threatening everything
Yet their twittering melted me…
Their thoughts a vine
Umbilical cords of threads entwined
I saw the childlike faces of my parents
Blinking into the sun
Cheering their saviour spitfires
Going out and coming in

I could hear their cartilage snap and creak
Like ribs and struts on canvas
With every flap an' wrestle of those
Mechanical strokes of airborne wing
Their fragile frameworks shaken

As they stubbornly pierce
Headlong winds
And all the traffic there
On escape to Africare
Their long forked tail-planes
Steering them
Computered signals
Linked by threads of vessels
To the navigating brain
Like tiny articulated planes…
… Could feel their minute
Thumping scarlet hearts
Beats a clock
Counting down
The remainder
Of their allotted time…
And on another
Though relative scale
Yet none the less
Inexorable…
Mine.

The Song of the Wind

Further than the view: The Dusty Path, The Windy tree
that song plays on and on and on inoffensively
it takes my time humming blind
and somewhere out beyond us find
we can see
that dusty path and windy tree
the landscape falls away so you can feel
what led you and me to the greatest view
that great blue yonder
and always it links my arm round you begrudgingly
for I was young and felt you were not for me
and it winds through my mind
of salad days they call them
in the midst of time
when I was indeed as green as lime

and once I went and climbed that tree
as you sat nervous laughingly beneath
I said to you can you see me
your mouth was wider than a smile
when you called up to me if I could see
any further than the view

And surely in life as compromise has led
to change the down with in my bed
I rage at no one else but me
for arrogance so categorically
that I once thought I was above
and you not good enough for me
and now tears hence you've gone elsewhere
but I remember how the wind played this song
in your hair
and in that tree as I climbed up there nervously
and how you laughed at a young me
at how silly I could be to take your love so lightly
to try and climb a tree to see further than that view

Rastrophiliopustrocity and the Horse's Head
The Sculpting Of A Horse's Head Called The Otter

In a stream and not in a dream
Alive in broad daylight
I saw an otter dive
A piece of oak from whence it squat
It regarded me then took flight
An instant could transpose for
It was there then it was not.

I kept watch til it was out of sight
Save a line of bubbles playing in its wake
And from the place with majestic grace and poise
While ripples still ricocheted from bank to bank
I saw an equine silhouette awaken tread furiously
Race up from the stream bed
From whence the otter sank

Burst through the surface
A geezer proud threw off its shroud
A brunette maned mare tossed
And pawed the foam flung air
Leapt and fizzled wet and sparkling
Her roasted chestnut eyes glowed red
But as in some silent film glanced terrifyingly at me
Down her flaring nostrils fled
Galloped off across another plain
Without a noise.

For hours I fashioned in a frenzy with chisel and mallet
In such a sweat – my head spun I saw my own blood
Like in a glass of violent shaken claret
Til at length I realised I shall not
Improve the form at all for
Time was against me.

Then from behind me heard the far off call
"Your work is done sculptor your work is done!"
A large heavy cloud that billowed overhead
Pursed its lips and said
"The horse is not all yours, its body sped away
And you are left only with this head!"

As the wood dried
The musky scent of otter went
I hung over the work
Collapsed
Spent.

A Sad Song – A Lament

One day at Crookwood as I bent
Digging through a heavy loam
A bird was singing a sad song a lament
And a feeling there and a scent
Caught me and chilled me to the very bone.
I looked up and round but nothing
Save a strand nay whisp of long hair there
On the ground on the mound I'd built
And one lone tiny footstep where
Should be two imprinted in the tilth.

Though surely I felt in the air beyond
A doubt someone was near
Never did I see or hear them close the gate
Nor did I see them turn the bends
Up the hill and away by track
On up the straight by Gordon Straker's stack

I met Barry Hunter the keeper later
The following morning – a liar he is not
He told me that the previous day as he sat
Eating bread and cheese, yawning
And waiting for a shot
He espied a shadow of he thought a girl
A silhouette walking lightly up my track
And where he thought I'd be, so let it lay!?
To later tease me for some craic.
But when he focused his binoculars
The image vanished in the hazy light
And where he'd gauged she'd be
A bird flew sudden in a state of fright
"It caused such a start in me!"

And I read it in his face
He fired off his gun abruptly
In reaction and it dropped
And when he and his dog went up to meet
It was then he noticed missing one of its feet!?

Of course there is coincidence and some
May well see sensation in our prediction
There is a fact in life that states
Reality's as strange as fiction
Now whether you believe his tale
Or whether you do not
The odd thing is that I was near
And never heard his shot!?

The Magical Mystical Avesbury Hare

It was March closing on April
In a Scamper
Two Hares released from a hamper
To the baying throng the song and cry
Release the dogs – stand by!…

The far off cries drifted like a shroud
Over Silbury hill
Across the downs a different pill
The night was cold and still
And in Avebury ring

Still not warm enough for Spring
Shepherds had put the sheep to lamb
Amongst those symbolic monoliths
And on the wing buzzards and red tailed kites
Began their circling

Below as night left day
The henge began its mystic play
The leverette stretched up from its steaming form
Shooting stars, one or two descending like fireworks do
Without a sound
Were eaten by the glowing ground
And emanating from the moon and far off sea
Sparkled silver on the frosted pasture
And caused the young hare's eyes to gleam
Moonbeams
They were everywhere
And piercing through the misty low-lying air
Like spotlights in and out the boxing hares
Who pranced and fought like manic gnomes in
Spiral patterns
Some directed spectred paths of runes
Celtic charms dancing on a bracelet
Of ancient stones

Mark Whelehan

The Hunted Fox

Between the lines I read the brief
Stepping outside the fallen fence
I saw inside the box
I touched the grief
Looking back the panting fox
Eclipsing his darkening hole
Stared unblinking right inside my soul

Below the scrub beneath the heath
He stole… neath weed
And wild flowers his wayside wreath
He crept collapsed and spent

The riders drew up like spiders
And on his shoulder
Came the hounds
I felt a criminal surge
For I said not a word
And though florid and rabid mouthed
They whipped reined in and urged me
A hushed and trembling finger
Pushed the lips of thought

My conscience fought
For he had killed my fowl before
But much as I wrestled
Much as I denied this
He was to me
Another cold and hungry creature
Alive and on this planet
With as much right as I
Like me wishing to be let be
Just trying to get by!?

Toby

In bed and nodding off one night
I put my hand out to stroke his head
Forgetting it was some years now since he'd been dead
Whatever that means.

He is still real to me because we had a bond
And something special
Signs that cannot pass away and separate
Two creatures minds.

I remember climbing til I felt my lungs would break
Me and my beagle hound far below felt and heard
The train go by which made the ground shake
Through roots and mist and hazy sun
Where fox's gloves and gossamer webs were spun
Slipped on dewy steps which long ago
Were made and clung to tufts and weeds and nettles stung
And briars scratched and thistles pricked
And hawthorn blackthorn stabbed and ripped
And when I grabbed his tail he growled
And when he nipped my heels I swore
And up and further up we tore
'til on our par a buzzard soared
We looked back down we drew blew and panted
He lay on his back and kicked and ranted
While I dragged him to my side
And we both fell silent as we sat
In awe at the rewarding view
How the hell we got back down
As that fog descended we never knew
But the bond between us strengthened
Into love respect and something true.

It held us in great stead that walk
And often when I think back
I see clearly how in life the path I trod
Became an uphill climb sometimes
But when I had attained my aim
With the help of some true friend
Was able to enjoy and
Share from there the view.

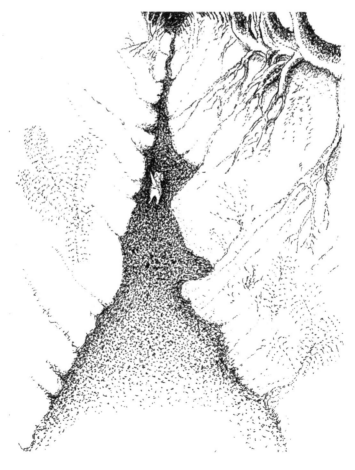

The Rocket

This is a story that unfolds
Maybe not in sequent oriented told
It is true… bold
And assuming – presumptuous even
When read in the cold
Light of day – say wintertime!
Something lacking in its cadence
May procure a tale too dense
It might not mean a thing
But coincidence it certainly does bring
And in its residue remains
The rusty memory of some thing
Once bearing original substance
What I'm trying to say's
That lots of things link up in life
Not everything is random and stray

Once upon a sunny day
A child and mother play
Splashing laughing in a stream
Like the sequence in a dream
Before the beast arrives

This perfect setting only letting
Sun to enter in on water dappled
By a giant overhanging oak
And hazel coppice cut back to free
And stop it choking light
I suppose you could say
The beast was me
But I only saw this scene
In a tiny photograph she sent me
Still I had been there
Many times and never seen
The Rocket

Yet I was searching up
The shore the day before
And searching in my pocket
My phone had messaged me
It was her…
Right there and then
I found a trunk of some wood
Paired by time and peeled
By the constant lapping tongue
Of water long gone but still coming on
I kicked it with my boot…
Rent its sepulchral tomb and vault

Which knocked off some root
It had evolved into a sculpted pole
Nestled in to hold the bank
Shored up and stole so deep
Into the clay to take it away
Would cause the bank
To tumble
How I pushed and shoved
This colossal piece invasive
Crayfish scattered mud and
Nettles briars splattered
The bank subsided and collapsed
An' I relapsed as well
My disc so near to prolapsing
Up the slippery bank
Back sliding many times
So waterlogged the hulk
But like Bruce's spider crawled up
I skulked sulked and sank into despair
Til with a mighty spine renting burst
Summoned up the energy
And surfaced it there
At last the summit onto track
And balanced with my rover limped it back

I told her the story on the phone and
While working on the wood
Her soft cajoling tone
As I worked alone made me
Feel a laughing Jackass
And indeed I looked down
And that is what I'd fashioned
And in a passion so set hard to
The task of metamorphose
Into a racehorse fit of course to reach the sky
[Of course] The Rocket

When burnishing its nose
I remembered booting it so rudely
So I use the polish used on it
Which crudely dealt the blow
To make a bloom upon its angry face
To absolve my sin
And show it now
Some respect and grace
… So now it is jet black

Looking back… In between we were beset
By violent storms which humble
Man and kind
Which echoes still the rumble
It was days later that I find when I knew
My visitors
Had been to play
That I saw in the photograph she sent
At the same place… I took stock[I tumbled it!]
It's there beside their splashing feet
The sculpture
I now have on my mantle piece
The pictures in my pocket
… Of The Rocket.

Cheval de Mer

I went up beside the wood
That drew a sculpture from my mind
In and out I searched in vain
Yet to me exciting times

Then I found a fallen tree with
Features in the oaken grain
It all starts over like a frame
Of film behind my eyes again

My head works within the mixture
Tangibly to find a texture
And always I feel this insane
But its only how I can explain

I busy myself with breaking clear
And cleaning rotten bits away
Suddenly there appeared
The horse I'd seen the other day
It wriggled from its coat of skin
And met the water in it swam
And like a giant snake it sped
And off across the ocean bed

Lost at sea I thought but then
It doubled back and like
A dolphin leapt high in the air
Again and again and again
Then its mane began to grow
And grew its very length
From head to toe
But no limbs appeared
Just fins and tails
No hoof-like nails
Its tail did swish
Almost like a jelly fish

In a horizontal plane it lay
Til I came back another day
And barely did I draw a breath til
I had worked as near to death as I could stand
My energy pulled me through of course
This is my work I always knew somehow
My hands would cramp and
It would drive me mad and fevered drawn
My palm so damp across my brow
So thrilled was I to work on this sea born
Horse L'Hyppocampe.

I am writing and putting the final coats
On this – varnishing the wood as dry as oats
Looking
Out from a room cocooned
It is not my day.
Curled up like dry seaweed budding
I am cut off windowed unblooding
From the sun and surf clouds scudding
Just a film spool revolving in front of me
Drop relegate merely the tool
Its effect an' cause
It belongs to the seahorse.

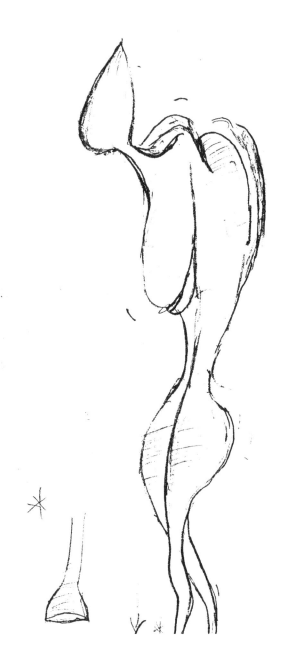

44

Mark Whelehan

An Alien in the Woods

I crept up through the silent wood
Where birdsong stopped upon my tread
And glimpsed ahead an oaken glade
An endless hazy bluebell bed

The twigs and branches snapped
Old and dry so long no one was there
Where underneath while badger slept
In between the fox had fled

A pheasants golden feather quivered
Where delivered grace like plume some fight
A blood drop fell and though I shivered
Knew t' assume no more than common sight

I felt the pang of sadness
No earthling would presume it rare to stand
But from another planet a traveller would
Be awe struck by this marvellous-varied fecund land

I walked along from this day on
Have stopped so often as is a plan
To wonder at these sights at hand
As if I'm from some alien land

And take back pictures not believed
To barren planet we can't conceive
To witness when they claw to see
The faces on my family.

The Climb (Along This Lane)

Who would believe me
If I told this tale out loud
Who would not think there is not a shroud
Of truth in it as so outlandish does it seem
That I so high up had not my feet upon the ground
And fell and then got up so safe and sound to scheme
To slip so far and down the mountainside
And come to no more than little grief besides
To some would think of me beguile and no surprise
To quietly secrete it in a poems guise
Artistic license does provide some breadth with stealth
So I won't relate it to you without a bill of health

Even when I started out along this quiet lane I felt
I heard a shout
As if in pain – And a shadow stalking me like an empty
shroud a monk
My catholic conscience haunting me no doubt
As drunk the night before
The hood had sunk as if it frowned its head cast down
Followed me around and out the door
As was the sun so bright
But thought I'd left it out of sight
As I lengthened my stride toward Helm Crag
Round and round and round I puffed
The path spiralled up to the crest my mind did lag
But no flag to mark it from frustrating bluffs
I thought my heart would bust with strain
I took my breath and huffed n' puffed slower slower like
Those old steam trains
Somewhere near some herb attacked my senses
Then I remembered what those old anglers used to say
When I caught the princess of the stream one day
'Thymallus Thymallus, they smell of thyme when
first caught!'

And this twigged in my thoughts its their latin name
They mistook it for the latin for the herb
Nor could they conjugate a verb
Thymum for thyme – waits for no man tempus fugit
And I could've broken the spell by correcting them was futile
And so by not I changed from boy to man
That day by keeping my counsel a tactful plan
But what the hell why spoil their stories
It was not about the smell t'was netting glories
The Grayling fish I meant and then I dreamt
I saw the acuity of play – landing the
Silver flanked beauty on the bank the cognoscenti say
It possesses a flamboyant red and blue
Spotted fin and a glittering shank of muscle thin and fleet
From pan to dish outdoors it tasted sweet
I used to be a fisherman and trapper I suppose
I sank unto my toes with praise and drank some sloe gin
And then regained my feet and off again
Happy happy happy days
How beguiling on the Wylie

My head began to rhyme a paean of praise for the great poet
Wouldn't you know it I'm sure the monk woke me
With a shove in my dorsal fin
Some reminder of a sin so with set grin not smiling though
Tore off my shirt put on a spurt
I rose as if through different climes to show
Like a fish from gravelly bottom through
Tickling weed to pop through surface skin
As cloud hung round the mountains side
I heard the Grasmere church clock chime below
More fiendish clouds of midges bit my fevered brow
So to escape them waved and blew and on the stroke a
voice spoke
'You'd better get a wiggle on t'is well past nine!'
The whip to crack
 'I Know! I know!' I shouted back

Was like puncturing some gossamer hide
Sweeping that fog aside
Sometimes sun mist rain then sun then mist again
Beside me as I raced along like a blackbird scuttling
twixt bush
Singing an ecclesiastical song
Until I reached the top where misty droplets
Dowsed to crack my steaming form I couldn't stop lest
Or he with holy water if still there absolved my
chastised back
And stared deep into my soul from out his sack cloth habit
Indeed I had that feeling of don't look back at it

The leaves were robin-red and white and golden brown
Orange yellow – all interlaced placed down as if by hand
Layers on layers before I reached the top
They had all once graced the summer trees
Like that liquid birds voice falling patinas
Next the gushing toppling ghyll smoking like damp fire
Spirraling like threads of condensing wire

Fallen since the hoar that bore the separation
Of their autumnal souls which every year I rue
The gilded bronzed embued burned and dappled pales
Of those ephemeral hues fell silently to earth
Glided down across the slides and skrees
Thus a gouache painted moutainside
Lots of chestnut beech oak and sycamore trees
Higher up rowan birch and pine shed theirs too
Now compounded squashed squeezed held in glue
And when depressed the footing made deep holes
T'was difficult to climb the mould yet eased my aching soles
So untouched this height from usual track
To make the soft earth underneath had
Taken years of stacking leaves
The damp the sound the touch the taste the smell
A breeze refreshed on this enigmatic fell
 But died and left a puff of cloud at summits face
I saw the buzzard buffeted circling
 Like an angel shaking look down below to scan the dell
Yet how hollow still the air upon this hallowed place

I stopped a few times in pools dug for animals to dip or water
Though crisp and sharp the air my thirst was great
Just to launch some over my arms and head did sate
 And therein lay a blurred reflection of my ageing face
All whiskered distant in that half frozen state
As if my face was looking through a plate at fate
Not back at me but through my present state
My self seemed to be searching for
The reasons I was there looking me up and down
As I looked back at it the same!?
And so it was while playing this identity game
 I thought love isn't kind to me no more
Just as this reverie took hold
Something shook me from its fold…
A dark shape retreated faded on reflection in this pool
And shivers sent to me so cool it rippled within
Had somethin' or someone backed away so thin
Was that evaporating monk scolding going to stay
Was it just my shadow while standing on that shelf
Saying,"Get a grip of yourself!"

A sheep's bleat far off added lonely charm
A sham I know as I spread out my arm
To trace and encompass misty views
But treacherous terrain as in vain
I realised I was a loner and no one else to show
A raven circled ominously they say they know
Croaking over craggy rock outcrops that grow
Inviting me to fall and dramatise the show
And plop like a rain drop into that tarn far away
And far below.

I keep my cool and drink the pure
When there and then I see a shape of something
Small and cream its form rise and fall in bracken scrub
It breathes – and make it out to be a lamb
In some distress its call a wheeze
It must be choked and cannot call its parent
To assist and must've fallen foul in that now rising mist
As I lurch and trip to descend to where it is
I see the raven fall like a stone to where it lays
I hear a groan and then a tussle

I tense every muscle in me and giant leap to where
I thought the sheep had lain

But as I land I find more than I'd bargained for
For here a fox caught in a gin-trap while stalking this
poor lamb
Incurred such mishap but starving was loathe to leave its prey
Had half struggled free and set its jaws about its tender throat
The ever opportunist raven was pecking at them both
And with sharp twist of beak had torn
At their eyes in a frenzied paroxysm
And as I raised myself from landing
Struck the raven with a blow
To emphasise our schism
It fell on me stunned still its tallons gripped my shirt
I sunk back in a grip of pain as my ankle stuck
Somehow in the gin – it gave I bowed
And cried out more shocked than injured with the hurt

I thrust out my hand to save myself
From slipping o'er the edge was sure
I glimpsed a black cloak I choked with fear
Falling back in my hand I clutched a turf of sedge
I launched it as backwards I did fall upon
The writhing sheep and fox who both let out a yell
The sod hit the desperate mother of the lamb
Whom unbeknown to me had heard its call
And to its rescue ran
The ewe slipped and tumbled forward o'er the crop of rocks
So landing on top of me the raven and the lamb and fox!

How could one decipher this sequence of events
Unless it happened all at once and one was
Sat alone in silence
So my mind a blur it did not concur
Til later what had transpired then and there
Stunned and all alive each one got right alone
I extricated from the trap my foot a gory mess
My thick boots saving bone
The fox behaving let go the lamb which fled
The raven flapped free of me only one wing torn
The ewe got up and nursed its bleating ward

No lasting damage to their eyes I saw
Just scratches, cuts to them so too the ewe and me!

And now I think of it
It's often raised a smile as I looked back that day
While resting on a homeward stiIe along this lane
Looking up at that distant crag
The picture of the scene must've been a thing to see
Each one limping off on their respective journeys
To beaten path and home to cottage hearth and dwell
To fell track and skulk to lick its wounds in lair
To gather with the flock for welcome warmth
To soar back to its summit's safety in the air.

 But it only very recently crossed my mind
When on a further climb I caught my hind foot
In barbed wire and in some pain my thoughts climbed –
and higher put
I wondered at him who set that trap the day this transpired
For what gain and maybe if they'd seen the mayhem
it had done
Some old poacher mates of past would sit in pub
snear and titter
Knowing me to be such a bullshitter
And although I was this day the mishapper
Had often in my past been an opportunist trapper
Would the monastery of my jury pull back their hoods
Bend their napes scratch their balding pates
And lean their counsel for this chancer
Hear Michael Angelo's refrain Ancora Imparo as their answer
If it was that monk I felt was there – did he wince in pain
With guilt for was it sane – was it shame – what was his
raison d'etre?
Or was he my alter ego telling me at every bend
and twist and turn
My life is short – my past I'd burn.
"We must get on you must get on!
You will forever learn… along this lane
Beware of doing it again!'

My Hat & The Fox

I went back to the place where we had sat many times [occa-
sions]
Just in case I found something I had lost back then –
Which helped my persuasion in
Looking for a hat
And that was my excuse for re-visiting
The scene of my emotional crimes
But in fact I had lied so often to you to play hard to get
My tongue so loose
At length in all those webs I wove I got found out
And you escaped my noose
And its only age makes me regret
As I have never found another
So really I returned with the daft thought of
Re-finding my old lover!

Anyway as I tooled around half contemptuously
There I found someone else's hat
A faded velvet riding hat
And thought maybe this place to be
Frequented by lovers from elsewhere
I sat and mused a while just there
And while noticing in the hat was caught
Some strawberry blonde strands of hair
From the hollow of a tree came a curious sound
And something moved and was watching me
It made no more sound so I decided to surprise it
And threw a stick
And hit the trunk wherein it hid
And pigeons sped away in fright
And my heart leapt and sank and I felt sick
All at once a voice emanated from inside
And shocked me instead
It was a low purr a steady panting that vibrated
It entered in my soul and said
And spoke of my passed times caught in love

And made me gasp
I sank onto my knees and held my head
Was such a hold the voice had on me
Though no matter what I try
A cloud descended of eerie mist and out of it leapt
A redheaded lady seated on a chestnut mare
Just like my ex love in hunting fare
She asked what I was doing there
I told her I was searching for a lost hat
She said she was the same
I proffered the one I
That moment found
She took it from me without sound
But leapt from the horse and pulled me to her
As we fell forever to the floor
I awoke to find her gone and nothing there at all
But heard a sound and looked around
And from the tree
A marmalade ginger vixen fox looked down at me
With yellow-green eyes
That pierced my soul with hypnotic gaze
Then barked and spat and hissed and sprang off out of sight
That's when I saw my hat behind the tree where we had sat
And when I called after it a distant voice replied
'We both have found our hats
Now take yours and go and never come back!'

The Story of Old Grey Billy & The Neophyte

So to palliate the pain I took some novacain
My tooth so bad
I went out some say stupid in the rain
With risk to catch a cold
Metaphorically because the track to the wood
So slippery all years leaves there tipped
And unsure underfoot
I had slipped up so many times and scolded afore
I was still young and vain despite my age
I had not turned the page
And was still learning

As I headed toward the wood
I heard a noise of something should
Be fighting against itself
In irritated whelps not engaged with other combatant
It was that same old boar badger
I used to watch with friends
When we neophytes learnt wind direction
How to stalk
Where to hide and not to fright
Playing with his family about their earthworks of a night
Under the roots of an old oak as we never spoke for fear
Of scaring these old shire folk…
His eyes and hide now almost white –
Caught against the gate spokes
The rear leg snagged in a loop and in a state
While darting through the pheasant coops
I hadn't seen Old Billy for a while and thought him dead
As many months before I'd witnessed a scene that
I'd never seen and for hours a fight ensued
Fought tooth and nail with the farm dog Jack
That epic spat had ended with neither giving in

The grunting whining growling shuffles forth and back
I with a stout stick refereeing as best I could
For as much I tried I couldn't prise between the two
In case they tripped me on my back and in their way
And tore to pieces in their attack
I shouted at them both til I was hoarse
But they wouldn't stop of course
One so old and sore he had nowt to lose
The other young stubborn and stupid to his cause
Jack was a rookie raw a neophyte
I recognised my old self in him
And so full of vim and fight
Full of testosterone contumacious vigour
Though gentle with a child was untrained and lary
He chased and killed anything wild and hairy
He was half choc Labrador and Staffy
And the latter made him a fighter relentless
Hard in jaw not soft but robust daft and sassy

The noise and bedlam
As if to cause a shroud was greeted
By a thunderous grey
And smokin' apocalyptic cloud
Above the towering oak trees
Surrounding arena-like the Ham Orchard
Crookwood
This awesome bout went on til like in hell
The barks screams and bells
The sky cracked and like a crimson gel
Seeped through – bled through appropriately
A single brief opening – a blinking
Broken eye in the evening sky
Then all fell black

A sunset to remember and the two animals wont forget
Jack ran off his swollen tail between his legs – his ruffled back
Sore bore many bites and rips this neo-fighter
While the wily old grey white eyed badger half blind torn and
Limping retreated into a briar patch to lick his wounds
Where Jack had roused him earlier sleeping sound
… Me I was exhausted and homeward bound

Paucity of habitat forced to be a maverick
So ancient and renowned was he
And now sick without best senses
Old Grey Billy he was called
He lived above the ground now
With the culling here
On his own had lost his cette and sow
To compound his plight yet to confound
He could dig no more – tempus fugit had seen
His sight his teeth and now his claws recede

Blunt from old age but still tenacious
This sage still had over time learnt some tricks
And was still a dangerous adversary to pick
So til his end.
So I set to, to free this creature I admired
Though knew a lot would not be happy with my act
Would rather tip the weary soul into a sack and
End his 'misery' there and then with a sharp tap
But I had envisaged for this old friend
A more convivial positive end

I reckoned he also may be plagued
And so his temper caused
By arthritis and toothache just like me
So for his sake left game regularly and paused
At his deep briar bed – of its whereabouts
Knew only me and Jack
It laced with my dental medicine
To aid his aches and throbbing head

I often see him ambling in my torch light walks
He only stalks the earth worms now
But often he looks up when I go by
A glint of something in his dull whitened eye
Is it thanks as if to say
"For setting me free that day
An' for easing my temper aches and
Constrains with that crumbled pill
So that my last days may be less painful!"

Of course I often see old Jack too
Who now calmer in character
As usual digs out holes and chases
Deer squirrels and rabbits for the craic
But if I teasingly sometimes
Shout " Where is Old Grey Billy then!?"
He turns about and barks
And whines – and always he
Looks sharply o'er his back.

Under the Golden Moon

I can't remember how long it took
Every day the feeling lessened
As my lesson in life
Increased like within my book
It is the same for everyone
Whose lost a love or was forsaken
Like falling from a tree into a brook
You land and you get up wet
And from a dream awaken
But you can see how far up you'd
Actually climbed and been taken

But while ascending so gradually
Never gauged the height
I'd drunk myself to standstill and my liver
It was as if I lived within a cage my plight
Routinal safe predictable caught
Just like my pet bird she does and says
What I tell her
She lives in whatever reality you give her
And she has no flight in sight delivered

So as time inexorably rolls on
I promised myself I'd
Keep my feet now firmly on the ground
And would not be tempted by anon
Any sirens' sound
So I took to walking out alone at night
Away from town noise and polluting light
Deep in beaucolic wolds
To set my thoughts away from love
I went out one night innocent as a child
For I knew little of the countryside at night
And called the owls to talk to me

And when the moon was like a golden cheese
And pipistrelle bats like flying mice
Flew through my thoughts to please
I forgot about my lovers' plight – things eased

I stripped off and howled back like a wolf
At all around my years of
Pent up anxiety released
Down a sunken lane I followed my sound
It echoed and went underground neath giant
Oaks which towered overhead

I felt their shed of floating leaves brush my soul
There was an answer to my call
I felt the world and felt its spin
I tripped on gnarled roots when
I looked into that haunting gloom
Like elephants heads
Stared back in that half golden moon

Watching me with one eye and half
Asleep and on one side they moved a touch
I bolted like a shot – electric hairs
All tingling 'long my form
And careering down the Folly slope I gave up hope
Of stopping but the cliff gave way I lost the trail
And must've fallen down a hole or lair
The woken pachoderms trundling at my tail

For when 'I' woke I'd dived – from head to foot
Was covered in its soil as black as soot regaled
And something wailed and flew past
I heard myself shout 'Shhhh!'
A flash of teeth and eyes I saw at last

After that I made myself some light
By which to see what I would have to fight
But it was gone my box of matches were all damp
I told myself to next time bring a lamp
Talking near a wooden gate I climbed up
No one with me so I wondered who I thought I'd spoken to

And that is when I heard an enigmatic whistle
Carry across the steaming field all topped with thistle
Down like a floss crested cloud had descended so quietly
This curious high pitched sound ripped through the
misty pasture
Seemed to cut a swathe through now airborne
Parachuting seeds
And brought me to the ground in deed
To kneel in pungent cow's plaster

I crouched I saw a dark shape it
Seemed to stalk some prey it had spotted
It crawled and trotted stopped and seemed to crawl again
At first I didn't know a stream was by the fence
But this creature on its belly slipped into some water thence
Because I heard the splash and felt the reverberations reach
Of some screech of fowl and then it beached
I thought that I ought to watch where I wandered from
here on
For I heard the crunch of bones and rip of flesh

As if I were in the water too I felt its chill and thought of you
All the memories flooded back as on incoming tides
That accumulate and soon have drowned
What's on their underside
Its back again I wrestled with the pain
That overwhelmed all my senses once again.

But hang on! As I reasoned with the thing
I had not been trampled on to death by elephanting
Nor dragged slithering across a marsh unto a dragons den
I'd learnt a lot and that though I was still panting
I started to whistle and euphoric tones ensued again
As I walked off home alone my life imbued excited

Though contrived this walk on the wild side
I'd endured and yet survived
My now full intent to join the regiment
Of those who let their caged birds free
And as I've now found an escape I want no hypocrisy
So she can sometimes feel she's free as a bird
Although caged awhile as free as me.

The Speckled Wood

for Helen

Though surely as I felt in the air someone there
I didn't see them just a misty glow emanating where
They had stood near this glade by Potterne Woods.
I thought I heard them click and open the gate
Nor did I see them turn the bend and up the sunken lane
But heard their soft tread and lightly leap over the stile.
For here is where Helen's ashes are lain a while.
I looked up and round but nothing there save a shy doe deer
And a butterfly, the sun burned through the sky
And beamed a radiant warm pattern on the ground
This little angel soft and brown fluttered down
Where I stood, it was her favourite… The Speckled Wood
… And is often there when I think of her.

Like in a Play of Words

Looking down from One Tree hill
And through Potterne woods to an idyll
I can see through the stallion flanks – three skeletons
Of bare beech trees stood like trilithons now winter hangs
Here where everything is held in a grip of frosted
Crust just the butter sun melting sliding over weakly
Mires of trodden mud broken fences and fallen leaves

And where those once fecund timbers
Overlooked that summer scene below
Crookwood slumbers now hibernates to show
Some weary smoke spirals from warm hearths
Blown off across by south westerly prevailing
The vale is hollow with echoes from the past
Forlorn cows penned up for their seasonal repast
Like foghorns in a thick fog blast intermittent only
To neighbours all at sea who answer from
Their flooded marshes lonely only with crows

I always thought if I went out there some day
This scene would start just like a play somehow
And last forever as we lived in summer
Now the curtains drawn the audience hums
We enter on the actors some farming community
Chris Giddings and his
Motley family crew – the players Harris's and dog Jack
Are slaving over a hot breathing
Pasture mown new in a distant green sheen they steam

Unaware the creeping billowing-up leaden clouds
Entering stage right ominously expanding
These are characters from a comely goodly scene
Whether among oak tree sun or moon and streaming rain
Glistening they toil and laughing to be tossing hay again
Now airborne parachuting seeds and dozy thunder
Flies tickle their throats squeezed dry fed
By bread and cheese and easy on the cider bibes

Thin at first in amongst all this song of beaucolic bliss
A bang and clatter and roll of drums build
The thunder grows wreaking havoc like giant guns go
And all asundry sheep and cows awakened
Would run for shelter somehow

And I would be brought to my knees
Cowering under mighty trees
And calling to the lad who grabs
The ropes which will close the interval tabs
And wake him from his slumbering's
With straw in mouth off stage in wings

A butterfly phoenix back to front
Would fall into this heat
And flutter down dry untrounced
And as the storm passed it announced
As soon as it had started out
What was all the fuss about?

Once again the curtains parted
Swallows weaving in and out
Would make the audience clap and shout
A fox trot by with hen in mouth
Would make them hiss and boo no doubt

Then Oooohs! and Ahhhs as eerily after the deluge
A buzzard circles rising from the
Milky meadows mews its mournful cry
An early owl calls out loud grips – ripples through
The watching matinee crowd

Water vapour like dry ice hangs suspended over stream
Where a kingfisher breaks the dream in an iridescent gleam
Creeps across the stage where undefended
Stunned drunken mice crouch shivering forms
Of still shocked rabbits and doe deer's fawns

Silent twixt the beak and bite of critters in the copses
They would laugh and fall about
When they witness a lovers clout on
Adrian the farmers nephew
Kissed by the maid of easy virtue
Like the mist come down and set to
When she finds out his shirts wet through
She shoves him off his perch he falls off stile
Amongst cat calls they met awhile at Urchfont village hall

The rich diversity of jeers snorts and chortles
At the horsey chorus girls who coiffured and liveried well
Steer – mere mortals – with more balls and smells
Than the mounts they ride – over hedge the other side
The piebalds skewbalds black and tans
Gallop by the sting of dung
In their nostrils they have brung

It is the Avon hunt their practising ride out for
The metalled tattoo of horses footfalls disappear
Haunting taunting politically in the foggy dew
Off they gracefully canter through
In the audience wiping eyes and gradually light banter
Turns to applause – it dies down the curtain falls

Sure enough there starts the murmur
Of the queuing evening performers
They're filing out as more pile in
Anticipating the evening
What might the late performance bring
Smiling at past repartee

But I know they'll all have been
Captivated by what they've seen
And though director of the lot
I will bow to Nature for her creative plot.

The Robin

As the moon slides away for the rising sun
I am lying here in a morning gloom
And guard my face from the light of day
All I want is to hide away

Outside my window there's that smell of spring
A small bird singing
An amazing tune burgeoning
As I start to crying for my impending doom
I can't help thinking if I sang that tune
All my troubles would pour out through

The opened window
Sucked like smoke and out the room
Even though I'm a fully grown man
That little songbird is beyond my stand
Wish I could cradle it in my guilty hands
Absolve my soul of shenanigans

And let me privy to its masterplan
Guide me warm next its beating heart
That's the rhythm that would start our journey
Invert the time jar reverse the sand
And then carry me back to its native land

Its twisting tongue twines threads of silver
Liquid intense then softer til the
Strains intuited of my plight
Empathetic though I'm out of sight
Delicate crescendos tilt then fall
Singing the story of its very soul
Out in the darkness and the icy cold

Mark Whelehan

This is the story of a condemned guy
Oh why Oh why Oh why Oh why
Wish I'd met this songbird sooner
I might've turned out differently

And like the epiphany of a migraine lifting
Greeted by that morning sun
Sift my sins to find some goodness
Disclose my passions to the dying moon.

The Cove

A precipitous bleak and wintry after noon
The total antithesis of June
Sighing spluttering and blowing like an un-baffled exhaust
The withered claws of windscape scrape on tough wet ropes
And wires a soused and bitter Beltane tune
Around the rugged rocks are strewn like marooned wethers
A flurry of black feathers float

Buffeted the crow manages to alight somehow
Upon a sarsen stone and gain some purchase
And so deliver gravitas into a picnic that it has
On fallen lamb and carrion
Enigmatic harbinger
Because it is so often seen alone
Like some anthropomorphised gnome
Hiding in its blackened cowl it clings to stone
Accentuates the chill the howl of wind and soul
Of all who are made of flesh and bone

Entering Averbury's ring
And opening the third eye of sages
Upon this ancient scene as if by chance
It does balance the ages in its jet black eye
And into sight hove the stone-struck couple
Known here as 'The Cove'
And from their lofty countenance the centuries have riven
Thought and caught suspended petrified their given pose
They stand leaning into hurricane torrential rain
and blazing sun
Silently firing shots so pellucidly done
Pulses of psychic projectile clarity
Strum when rubbed with searching hand
And minds so proffered open
A tactile smoothness more potent than any mighty gun

Who are we to scoff who register no feeling
When we witness others feeding off a frenzy squealing
Stealing into huddles in summer baked or winter puddled
Such that they can't keep away and pray un-muddled things
There with such solemn issue entering
And absorbing into every tissue of their inner selfs
To hell with what they say [like teaching children
Don't believe in Father Christmas and his elfs]
Go out and grasp the day carpe deum is the word
Let cynics shy away

If not cracked up to all they be in sediment
These ground up stones in powdered shafted rays
Pummelled in some supernova element
Jettisoned in an earth-shock later sprays
The impenetrable vastness of space will be no impediment
In times hence shall stay potent and hold grace
Although not as we see them now we grant
And meet them face to face now as 'The Cove'
In forms of energy they will be as vigorous though so
very old
And to beings thence just as adamant.

Sweet Smoke

Dedicated to Chris Giddings, Crookwood

At an old cottage I passed the other day
Everything was done in the old way
There was an old small man turning old hay
Something quaint was within him no guile
He worked at a pace but with rhythm and style
It was thought provoking and made one smile
Rhubarb leaves shrivelled beet and parsnip shoots
Carrit roots old bedding plants all being tossed on a heap
Bean and raspberry canes and onions gone to seed all a'steep
Old asparagus, plum and apple, old cabbages walnut and
pear tree prunings
Pollarded branches of yew and quite a few
Verdigris encrusted oak branches and headed blooms
Working hard he never spoke he couldn't hear me if I clapped
Unless he saw me then he doffed his cap

Every so often he stopped to take air
Lifting his cap to a shock of white hair
That made you think of something elsewhere
His hearing aid whistled in the wind as he sorted it
His nosed dripped and his eyes watered
Like some morse code device he snorted at it
He wiped it it pipped and squeaked while he pressed it
deeper in his ear
No gloves upon his huge cracked gnarled and blackened
hands did he wear
While threw everything out of an old shed which drew mice
escaping to pastures new
Broken tea chests boxes packed and strewn about the pire
which grew
And scariest of all old rabbit skins like masks of
something pagan

Foxglove stalks and briar rolled bailings
All forked up – pigeon nests and tater peels
Creosoted planks with rusty nails – anything!
All sorts booted out

Setting them alight, wakened owls hooted
I could just make him out in his old clothes
His old boots and gaiters, his trousers patched
held up with string
Using his old hat like a bellows wafting smoke over
everything
As bats flew through and stars blinked open
And ash sprinkled in the air like snow
His bonfire climbed and the flames grew
And it roared so and smoke blew over me
And sparks too sprayed and landed
And on my clothes tiny holes made
But I knew him and that would do
That smoke came from the fruit of his labours
And from his very soul

No one minded least of all his neighbours
And it smelt the same from whence it came
It smelled so sweet that smoke it crept at first
Then billowed down the lane and burst
He was from kind and plain and gentle folk
And not broke but he didn't drink a lot
and deaf so he rarely spoke
But he would smile almost toothless at me
With a joyous twinkle in his eyes
Like the stars, like he knew, like he saw right through
And raised his hand as I strolled by
'Hello young man!' he shouted and I'd shout 'Hi!'

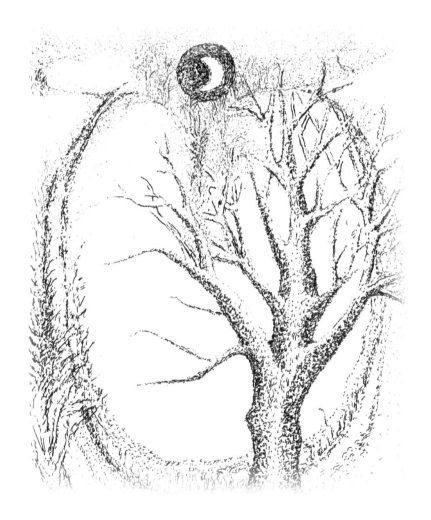

Parted

I crept to Crookwood stream one night
Where planets like alien eyes became
Watching me my heart inflamed
Beat loudly through the gate a size
Enough for me to squeeze through by
Hinges not impinging while
This stillness lasted late
Still I stopped to wait just thinking
Nervous that windows might illuminate
But when all is said and done
And though there's no one else about
My thoughts did scream and cry and shout

But not a sound did come
Save an electric interstellar hum
Complimented by the drum of water
Gushing through a funnel goaded
Tunnelled neath the metaled road
All would hear Jack's bark nearby
Ignite a murdering of crows
Huddled spectred shadows now
A catalyst for windblown horn
From cows to grow
All sounds different when its dark
Nothing at the farm alarmed
Broke the silence and the charm
No unusual noise
No feeling of invasion
No harm done on this occasion
I set off along to my liaison
A meeting with the sky
Midst blinking wrought by nova plumes
Some spluttering nebula out of tune
Reaching far off faded out
Roaring volcanic magma spouts

Anti-climaxed shrank to pout just throbbed
Fought black holes in showering fumes
My shout my panting breath consumed
Great rusty balls of iron loosened spheres
Unfettered liable groaning as old metal does
In amongst all that fuzz of neon light and strobic buzz
Clanged and sighed and grated yawned
Showering sparks on planets' dawned
Fated to collide in a large scale genocide
Huge ship hulks on collision course
Cannibal ballistic carnivores eating each other
Roaring greedy devouring maws steered by gravity
Rolling slowly out in space anonymous without a face
Loose cannons mavericks showing grace
Before they died in explosions of suicide
Gigantic ghosts their ogred silhouette
Chased to make me quicken pace and sweat
Camouflaged 'cept for three red lights
A triangular shadow
Slid across the snowdrops face

All this made my stomach sink it lucid took
The height looked down from in that ink
That I would drop if I could think how far
Those massive orbs if out of sync would fall
Pulled apart a cloudy nimbus curtain opened
The encrusted diamond sky driven by
A sudden solar wind I feel –
Aided south-westerlys 'cross the field
Eclipse over as cumulous swept away as well
A thousand galloping horses winged in flight
Their nostrils steaming leaving trails
Flairs ended with their vanishing tails
Explosions woke up racing hares
Badgers foxes sought their lairs
Already had me dreaming
As static charged my hair

Scrawled above hung all my schemes
Like broken Christmas baubled dreams
Those sprinkled thoughts displayed in verse
Some dark matter laid a curse
Lines 'cross pages written home
Some showers of shooting stars to wish on
Like parachuting seed to grow from
Blown from some child's dandelion

Seven Sisters Pleiades shone
Clustered near the northern shoulder
Still hanging bright as we grow older
Artemis and her lovers gone are now the prey of everyone
There on the celestial equator
Orion rested on his side
Northwards vain Cassiopeia reclining
Opened her arms out wide
With ageless beauty not denied she teased the hunter
Across the deep divide hurling meteors at his face
The Great Bear snarled but knew his place
He pushed his ursan plough through space
And winked at all this silliness
Yet glancing round his eye it feasted on
Cassiopeia lying eastward[s]

There winds a path along the stream
Where Snowdrops by the starlight gleamed
Revealed to me my journey along the bank I trod
But as I walked in circles I tripped upon a sod
Counting constellations I'd ignored my random way
I sank and drank it in, my god,
So silent made me whisper to myself
Suddenly I tumbled the heavens rumbled my contrivancy
They all tipped from their purchase there
As off a shelf slid sideways glared
Flew I sought of
Fell, tumbled to the floor and
Grounded inches from the water

I oughta had a bath
Startled a disgruntled hedgehog crossed my path
In awe soft leafed mould caught me though
The splendid stars revealed so beaux deep crisp so clear
My mouth stared upwards shaped an 'O'
Spellbound by that heavenly glow

So cold I had such thoughts though couldn't sleep
I munched and mulled on fallen plum
And apple bites and pears did gore
Til I couldn't hardly eat no more
Lasted there despite the hoar
Since autumn some to birds and rodents near
Some worms had bored many bitten to the core
Gobbled by soft tread shy deer
They lay like rubies opals sapphires emeralds
Scattered on the floor like some pre-Raphaelite horde
And all about enchanted smell
My fallen orchard dingley dell!

I leapt up crunched on frosted twigs
A silent owl glided by
And dropped its pellet by my side
I praised the lord that pigs can't fly I laughed
In the distance heard the train or was it a far off cry of pain
Brought me back to sombre muse again
But had no time to keep til dawn broke
When my sheep would yawn and bleat stroke their flax
The steam arising off their backs in spokes of sunlight
Eyes so creased with sleep like slits
So alone the shepherd sits then lays down slides
On his back looks up to contemplate an epiphanous birth
Drawn up at the sky again to smile wide
At all that overpowering sense of mirth
Of gold and myrrh and frankincense [olibanum]
I saw my total utter insignificance [in this agrandum]

So only as the milky way
Like snowdrops drifting aimlessly
Twisted as my stream did play
More a hazy churned lactating spray
I'm convinced I saw it turning yay!
And you were there
Groaning on its lonely axis
My wish and only hope to see you
Voyeuristically playing with my telescope!
Your home is there I would say

So cold you were your heart of snow
Though melted now I hope
Stretched and spiralled ran
From me far below those trillion billion suns
Far and away like you are now
Electric charged and still linked say
Misty white like turning frosted hay
A million million lightyears away
Some may say it's a fallacy
But God well knows it to be
That there are others out there
In this galaxy

And as the cosmos spun
I wished that one could cut loose
The bonds of love that dwindled
There beside the stream rekindled where
Water under bridge was gone and done
And dusted by those stars looking on
Was all so long ago drove men to drink
Tristes illicit mental rendezvous I think
Pulled and tormented their inner sides
Sunk down to earth with gravity drove
Eaten up with depravity hove and lies
Their souls tattooed with sins of coveted love

I fell to sleep I saw your face
Beckoning me into outer space
For ages aloft we spun as one
A twister unlike any brother and sister
Lips to ear we hummed our tune
As long as that cloud of stars winds on
And danced as tethered oh so late
It turned to rain, snowed blizzards,
Sun burned hot, frost bit
Not once did we separate

And although our time together
In the time of universe
Would hardly constitute a verse
In all the words ever written
About a love that's stricken
Yet in the blinking of that eye
For you I would have gladly died

Such hyperbole clichés used so many times of
And I perplexed soul with reason rhymed of
At length you pushed me away from you
Tears welled up with in those eyes but soon froze
Translucent impenetrable Ice green like a frozen lake
And you cried so say for my sake," I have this to say!"
You spoke and told me not to whine
But be a man and wait a time [I chose!]
Til you were free to choose or I shouldn't bother
So with that I thought there was a serious chance
I could lose you all together to another
And sure enough in that time lost you
To me an immeasurable cost to[o]

Thus as I trudge up by my stream
I trip and fall and shout and scream
I dream an interstellar theme
Of all the things I hold esteem for
And all the things in my short life
That haven't hurt me or gave strife
Very few remain for me save
Tinkling Snowdrops in my mind

And the milky way the way it winds
All planets and the stars that shine
In God's creation nature find
Her so thoughtful and so kind
With the holy Virgin birth
That star that came to save the earth

And as I walk I search I see
First acrospires of snowdrop free
Very soon they grow to be
And like the stars they shine through cloud
Through leaves and trees and scrubbery
Through mangled messes of humanity
A stretching mass of purity
Shining together oh so brightly
A string of pearls way out at sea
Forever they float back to me
And wherever I do roam
A thousand thousand miles from home
They walk with me constantly
And when I look up at the stars
And sometimes when I'm all alone
I dream of them in pubs and bars
Along that track I call my own
And although I know they know
Something that I'll never know
The parted Snowdrops virgin heads
Nod agreement in their beds

Though older now and not as bold
Still daunted – haunted by your form
Which masquerades as you so young
Which age has surely now undone
And memories of me now long gone
But once just like those heavenly lights
Intertwined we sparkled stellar bright
And no matter what or weather
We clung and sang and…
For a while… we shone
Together

The Vixen: So As You Will Be There

Just so as you will be there
I write this in a crispy air – lost a life
On Boxing Day nothing new there – you say
Hung in a larder to defrost the pheasant warms
Crunching crust of earth neath feet
 Trudging home dead beat
Wife waits husband for the meat

At all costs a mother brings up soft warm things
A yawn of satisfaction silent 'cept
The long canines clicked, snapped shut
A turn around and left a spore of defecation
Upon a steaming mound for your delectation
Eyes swept wide across the vale
 Nothing but beauty there prevailed

The Sun rolled out behind a lifted paw
Which thawed a melting winters maw
Giving the Fox a shadow and the trees
She digs out a nest of hibernating bees
Scant scran but it's taken to her cubs
She runs in the snow dark holes to her lair
She pauses outside to look round
Sifts for scents on the freezing air

The honey melted peppered stings
On her tongue she sneezed
The single hair from her nose falls down
She knows her brood were growing strong
Like dew drops sliding down a stem
She swallows alert and listening guarding them
And down her cavernous throat their song
It slid just like the falling sun went underground

It was then she realised the clouds swept in and
Golden gone the smell of blood was what was on!
She tasted it on the wind
And in that bay of hounds

It was distant a whisper led the hunt
As mother watched on
She whispered something blunt
Then she was gone
They passed they clip clopped one by one
I kept my gate closed even so
They nodded every one of them
Ending with one said Errrhemm!
The accent there just to condemn

And some of them so juvenile
Their pinkened faces jovial
Then the last one who I knew
It felt so impersonal
As if they led my funeral
Ending with the word errrhemm!
The accent there just to condemn

The entrance to the fox's lair
Was guarded by a single hair
Caught on the barb of a briar's thorn
Wafting in a breeze since dawn
Was she in or was she out the breath
Upon the huntsman's shout a hymn
Curled away and with her ran
Across the green and pleasant ground
Of Angerland, Jerusalem

I Used to Dream About the Sea

I used to dream about the sea
Of ideas swept away
But the tide turned
When life was learned
And they all rush back to me
And footprints webbed on the ebbtide showed
Disappeared on the full flood – clouds race
As the moon glowed and tugged waves obeyed and rose

Lonely foghorns haunting nights
And floating hands drummed upturned hulls
That broke the surface like rusted
Crustacean mollusc crusted whales and stalagmites
And identity once lusted now worn faded frail
Ephemeral letters S.O.S…
Written in sand with salt encrusted nails
Flown spume and then some
Of lost lover's sunken long gone
Last words to me

I used to dream about the sea
Its wholesomeness – depravity
Staring in grey waters there
A grey seal staring back at me
Where each enigmatic wave crashed
On the beach reverberate orgasmically
In the spokes of sunlight dying
Splashed orgies of such gravity

The gaps between the waves holding parity
Til parted by dividing wakes run aground
O'er shallow sand bars silly jokes
Like tiny fish are nibbling me
Were spookily prescient and gloat
How long could I hold my breath while others

Waded in to free their souls omniscient
And set their thoughts afloat

I used to dream about the sea
My barnacled bottomed brain
Washed up on a stormy weather vane
Spins round and round again
Racing horses ploughing furrows salty sailors we
Swim back to me
Don't leave me on this rock
This butter pladdy looking out to sea

Far out on the horizon my lover would be tossed
About and sinking I was always lost and thinking drinking
How I'd save she brigantine
The isthmus tethering our minds
The hardest thing in life to be
To make a bad decision

I used to dream about the sea
All at sea and floundering
Sink or swim all the clichés grounding pounding
Ricocheting back to me
Along the buffering breakwaters
Absorbing the crashing force
Off course of all we know to be
Holding on for dear life

We would live on happily enough with the bluff
Red herrings eaten talking guff
But then one day I'd have to say
My thoughts jumped ship and
All the boats just sailed away
The rats the crew fair-weather friends one and all
Left the sinking barque called 'ME'
The buoy became a man maybe!?

I used to dream about the sea
All childish hopes and dreams like drifters who won't stay
All my serious poems and dirges fade away
I could tell as that bottle thrown sank upside
And down in the great heaving swell
The seagulls flew– sped off as well
And silently sea sick
Without a mew puked up their catch as afterthought
With other fish to fry

I used to dream about the sea
My love too would never do
Or come true and in that message dwell
Seaweed climbed up and consumed the lighthouse
In whose ivory tower once I lit my lamp
My heart collapsed and tinder damp
No space too cramped for style
Even so turning back the clocks a while
I invited siren – like, weak souls unto my rocks

I too sank beneath the water's surface and in the clatter
Of the pebbles race and the great gasp of breath sucked
In by the ruinous teeth and back drawn current tore receding
Waves upon the screeching sliding shore so loud
Of sinking sand the hour glass bore and reaching out its
claw-like hand
To grappling grasp the rasp the reeper slipping not
holding fast my shivering dorsal fin
Before I return suffice to say inland to safe sheltered
lubber's paradisic bay
No sound now in the shell-like tunnel of my ear
of breaking seas on sand
Just the distant smoke breaking the ice white cloud
From a funnel disappearing in my head
Someone else's stoking fire presumed dead.

Paradise

This world at times
Drove me insane
I wasn't coming back again
In two thousand and fifteen
I felt in the world I'd seen
I had been if you know what I mean
Something hit me in a dream
And it was time to move on!
An epiphany awakened me
In some song I sang
I grabbed some clothes
And from my draw
A picture of the family
And friends I bore
Some scraps of food some string
And a pen-knife just in case

I sloped off down the watery lane at a pace
Only the lemon face of a watery moon
Accompanying me like a crocodile eye
Blinking in the shadows of
A billowing thunderous sky
Skeleton tops of trees scored
The underbelly of these clouds
And tore into their sunken heart which
Like mine was heavy and soon it bled
The rain came like a shower switched on
And as I tiptoed the clap was heard
And lightning strike like angry words
Drove a murder of angry crows
To chase me up a woodland trail

I raced twixt briar and nettles
And ripped my knees by thorned flayel
Uprooted frail bluebell petals bruised where they stood

Like a turquoise carpet trashed in the sour light
So when the paroxysm of fear of being
Struck pecked and getting wet subsided
I so deep in thought threaded slower
Through its platinum silhouettes
Collided with this vision and as I fell
In smokey mission some craft had landed
Some hand bid me stay with no words to say
Handed me a scroll and snatched it back
Which hieroglyphics on
And branded just the same this ship such things
As never had I seen before
I looked up as it disappeared with awe
Lifted myself from off the floor neath giant pine trees
Which left needles printed on my palms and yet
Strode on

Escape before too old my mantra
No look back o'er my shoulder
Off at a canter
This world at times drove me insane
I'm not going through all that again
Two forms wet through and dressed in black
Pointed me to go back
I reckoned I knew them not I have to say
And so stayed on my track away
And when I turned the bending road
Nothing of my past life showed me
Except the clothes I still had on
And a picture now of times long gone

I remember now the telephone
Sheltered in that red box shivering
Like a drowned and hunted fox dithering
Lifting the receiver cold as a buried bone
Heard a word beneath your breath
Only a hair's breadth away soft
Then the cancelled tone
Alone… you call that love?
The phone was dead
In my head the ticking clock
The door slammed shut

Every tread tick tock
My reckoning now to walk until I drop

Years it seemed had passed me by
When whiteness lit up ahead
Which led me onwards and I fed
Upon its glow so warm and soft
And spread out wide across a plain
Yet still I anchored on the lane
It was as if it snowed but it was chalk
Luminous in the purple blackness
Aircraft swooped tanks discharged earth lifting bombs
Almost buried in a tomb I laboured on
I was on this great plain bang! Another shell exploded then
This really was insane
Had circumnavigated great stones up o'er a hill
On passed gorse stunted copse of beech
In the wind ghostly groans of ancients speak
A massive henge rose into view then
must have doubled back again
The weather altered in the middle
after hasty windswept piddle
Suddenly from up above a soft explosion of burst pillows
Snow billowed all around
in half an hour was over ankle near shin deep
I tripped and tumbled over drowsy sheep
Great guns rumbled ravaged by lack of sleep
And for want of energy I made that place my bed
Digging out a hole with my bare freezing hands
Neath some vehicle like a sled
This world drove me insane
I was casting off the chains

It was neath a shepherd's hut I'd moored
Something poured ice cold down my back
Hoof hearted and Ice melted
I remember those words my father said
I laughed out loud then awakened
In my water bed
As I dried I tried to reckon on
The time but it was a blur
Spring had woken up as well and

Everywhere I smelt its smell occur
Starving I followed bees unto a hive
Lifted the lid and gingerly pulled
The wax aside and let the honey slide
Lifting the whole molten comb
And forcing in my mouth
It trickled down my throat

A hum grew growing to a savage roar
My god that's good but as I hung around
The bees in a furore swarmed over me
They went berserk was stung all over hands and face
And hide as I may they came back for me
And made me pay were so annoyed
And made me think differently of their work
I had destroyed
I'd learnt

So for many days I walked on like through a maze
Learning skills though in a daze just to survive
Through the suns haze and in a blaze of
Lucid thought made me gaze out
Miles away across this wide wide vale
I sat awhile and considered life and
All therein and in this window of pellucidity
Contemplated past miss demeanours and complicity
I might've wished those sins to be contrite must
Confess them to be light of their heaviness
And gain some credit from upstairs
And to gain absolvement from
Agreed with myself to speak them out
To every Tom Dick and harry
Who may foolishly tarry
By me

I walked beneath a blossom tree
A million cherry petals fell
Like seagulls out at sea
Floating over dips and swells
And fish held there like in some spell
And underneath so was I as spellbound
As these snowflakes fell

Across the oceans boil they float
Like countless white confetti
As many as the wildebeest
That roam the Serengeti
And with the scent of wet soil
In their bovine nostrils
Thousands of miles they trail
Following humus tills
Chasing rain and grasses
On their vast migration spills

Rain it spells hope
They taste it on their tonsils
With this far off thought in mind
Came invasions of an equine kind
Suddenly like a roar I felt
The hairs on my neck arise
A stampede of horses down the pasture came
Like waves crashing on the shore
They bore down on me and I tore
Through into a ravel of a tangled copse
They pawed the ground and rolled their manes
Their eyes rolled white insane
And screamed at the indignity
That they could not trample me
And nodded wildly as they sniffed me out
And though I shouted and waved they stayed
I smelt the smell of grass juice on their breath
As they peered into the shade of where I hid
Something slid by my feet a grass snake
And wakened by the stamping feet
Dodged through their lifting hooves
That was it – they were off
They bucked and kicked and
Free from bridle reign and bit
Galloped off making the most of it

Was redolent of everything which came to pass
Although religiously I did my daily ablutions
Washing in a stream was no way a solution
I must have looked an ass or worse
As they drew near they expected me to curse

Not grin and bend upon one knee and spurt out all my sins
Whom whoever met me on the road crossed over with fear
It was not my size I saw it in their eyes an animal they drew
When they glimpsed my mode I must've looked appalling
When one day I stooped in genuflexion
To consider my reflection in a puddle
I witnessed the tarred and weather beaten face
Recoiled with such distaste disgraced
In all that muddle of beard and hair
I walked like something feral
I crouched and stared from side to side
My eyes and teeth white as pearls
Not weary but electric with alacrity
And that was why I looked like that
And why they looked at me like that you see?

To find food I noticed it took imagination
The irritation of swollen feet due to threadbare socks
So missed and shoes' soles patched
With tin foil from walking over rocks
But I ignored all this pain as I harvested my tucker
Imagining that nuts and berries were to me high supper
And rich leaf mould and roadside herbs
Damp which soft filled my senses and my days
So near to villages I crept but never wept for wanton ways
And as curled up asleep with dry leaves for a blanket
Wet herbs stained my underneath always did I thank
My lucky stars that hung there pulsing overhead
Though bitter shock of nettle stung below the bed I mounted
Left mellow stains upon my soul so tired
The many spires of churches went by uncounted
And unentered
Always it seemed life teemed
A buzzard always overhead circling mewing
Like some lost stray cat I sometimes raised my fist at
And a whole list of familiar things that I felt contempt for
I'd anthropomorphised the bloody lot
I munched upon the crumbs I'd left
And with that knife tore off lengths of hair and beard
Which grew down to my feet quite white in places
Tempus fugit and all that
And crept and tripped me often that I feared it

Though my fall it softened
And jumble thefted from the hedges passed
Tucked it neath my clothes for warmth
Tied up with string to face anything
Still I strode on just years it felt
Just a walking tramp a cast off not of human race
Berating cows and sheep that stared
And anything which peaked at me
For I had no one else to speak to cept my paranoid self
And street lamps I dared to go and glow beneath
Spotlit my empty soul and the big hole in my humanity
As time did melt only
my metronomic footsteps kept time
Relentlessly down a hollow sounding corridor
Hiding and running escaping shunning
In my brain drained of sleep and food creating cunning and
A madness in me

I knew deep down below if I was respectful of their lives
Birds and creatures of the woods and fields
Would come out from their nests lairs and hives to say hello
Finches warblers tits hawks owls and sparrows
crows of every hue
As I mused of lies I'd wished absolvement from they knew
These creatures were not baggaged so must hold from
Issuing my blame on them
I had to bite and chew my tongue in annoyance
As a chiff-chaff warbler incessant in the bush or tree
Was ever the backcloth to a birdsong stew
But by god I missed it when I was away from it
And swallows red white and blue dived at flies
Which followed me would twitter and sing like anything
From their hearts instead not irritation
It spurred me on now… and butterflies
Landed on my clothes to rest and sun themselves
And blessed me with their opening and shutting wings
While I let the sun kiss my upturned face
They settled there and on my hair
And kissed me like lovers lashes do
I sat upon a stile a tiny bird flittered down
With grace and doffed his hat
T'was a blackcap

It's delicious warbled song though stopped abrupt
Dribbled through my ears and touched
The happiest I'd been so far for years to sense no guile
A sanity oasis for a while

One night giddy from no sleep and nourishment
The moon stole into view and climbed into an orchard
I lay down to ease my aching limbs and sate this lunar view
By greengage peach and apricot and apple fruits and pear
Everywhere the moonlight seemed to travel there
And soon not in years it spoke seductively dear lunar ball
Baked into a crust rusting up there dried out over all
These verdant orbs you lick with light which
make you lust for juice
Like green planets round a sun bring happiness to everyone
Hang and glow in stellar clusters sewn woven
Clouds of former worlds exploded from
Their tender loads on trembling limbs lit like
A thousand go signs on a road pendulous
In this orchard space stare back at your barren face
Hang a line of beacons for the swerving bats to come along
And as they invariably do
Rub the fruits as they pass through
Their sonic squeaking sound like mice
I was gripped by what ensued
The sweet nectar balls burst and split their engorged form
And trickled down and spread their seed where
in the morning
Swarms of manic bees and ants did feed from dusk til dawn

Your husk form pulls such tides
Which torments our insides
This cycle continuous as your moonshine is
But far beyond that single silver melt
Don't mistake this as a tear of agony
Dear moon you are the one lost out
As nothing burgeoning in your womb
You have nothing else to do but hang around and wait
Your turn as lights go out one by one
For when this sun burns out
So will you and me and the solar system
Flipped turn inside out

And every so often on that path relentless
I knelt to ask to whom I did not know
Who I was and whence I go lest this was pointless exercise
No answer ever came but still I struggled up and on again
Ached in body and in mind together
From bending roads and bloody swines of weather
It drove me insane

A million people crossing streets and climbing stairs
to nowhere
Fighting shouting to be heard this multiplied by ninety
The city scape the herds of Christians Muslims and the like
Kneeling down and praying to escape the urban plight
Always always always did I keep this in my sights
In case I lose my mind on these lonely starry nights

Glancing o'er a hedge one day I spied a couple in the hay
Laughing and cajoling they were happy
Rosy cheeked like apple blossom in April or
hawthorn in the May
As the larks that climbed on high this sunny day that
lashed its rays
They trilled and hearts leapt filled fell and climbed in natures
Rhythms swayed and squirmed like fishes in a pool
Cool and thrashed holding splashed like coiled eels
on migration may
Shyly did I slink away just like a fox who hovers with one
paw held still
Wants to stay
When he softens thoughts and sees the badgers play
But knows the hunt is on his heels and closing on their prey
So I left them to their day and whistled on my way
For curiosity killed the cat I thought or so they say!
Another of my schizophrenic lives gone by the by

Then at length I met a hill that climbed so high my breath
Was barely caught til I fought and crawled up to a crest
And peered over as best with semi blinded eyes
From days of sleepless nights
I glanced behind me as from a buzzards perch so high was I
At all my life the trail of my days now gone by
Back to that tiny town in the distance frowned

And blinked back at me in the sun
The road I took spun… I fell… I slept must've been four ages
For my hair had grown again
This world had driven me insane
There was No way back again

Shapes ahead became a farm with steaming staring cattle
But I didn't care through opened chains rattled on the gate
Which entered by I trod and swept aside
The grass was green on the other side
The sun kissed everything again
Licking gold and golden the skin of people laughing
As they waved at me
They were all insane

A young man came forward in his arms
He held out to me the top layer from an opened tin
A present for me… the simple bakes therein
I heard him say they only cost one pound fifty
So honoured I by they
I smiled at him he shifted shyly of his feet
He had honesty simplicity to meet. So sweet.
"That only cost you seventy five pence!"
I cried – he smiled abashed in eccentricity
A yellow eyed dog leapt up at me and licked my face
And barked and jumped and barked
For the biscuits I had or was it more
I grabbed his paws and danced round around
Mad mad mad!

One old man I seemed to know from years ago
approached me
As he pointed a crooked gnarled finger over my shoulder
He said, "You've gone full circle Markie. This is where
you started and this what you've come to pass alone
Won't do no good to roam 'tis time to build
And in the greater scheme of things the time you've killed
You're not that much older than this green
green grass of home… !

Only wiser I thought whatever that means
As I spun around and around and around

Til there was no sound of him or anything
I stopped and laughed and laughed
And laughed with them at the insanity of it all
Soon the spinning in my head stood still
But this time I didn't fall

It was then I knew this was to be
And wasn't dream but reality… sound
It was simply nice
This was the place I'd found
My home my land my ground
My paradise

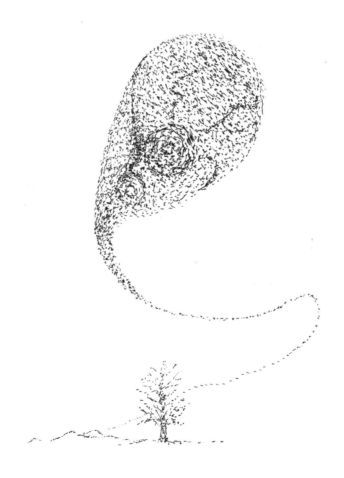

The Grey Wagtail

On this winter's day I made my way along a half flooded mud-
ded track
Trudged deep in a dream by a foaming stream which runs along
it's back
Whistling a song I couldn't shake – so strong the water break,
milky white – was gone unheard
A long streak of colour like a firework trail amongst the hoared
and browned
Tore through my comfort zone made me wobble in my stride at
the same time I heard my phone and hurriedly felt down search-
ing it before it stopped
Like the hole ripped through my side out which my heart
dropped
I tried to hide the news which scarred me on my own
A sapling grown across the spate of water somehow like a bridge
amongst a cloud of false wakened midges which shouldn't ough-
ta be there in this winter air
All other sound deep and drowned did bottle
thoughts profound
Fused in that roar had news of a departed friend in the fore been
true did gloom
But before I knew, again a grey and yellow bird was suddenly up
alighted
As if a discarded letter squeezed into a ball in rage lit and thrown
through a darkened room burnt out to reveal the phoenix as an
angel
Swaying with momentum on its purchase stroke its plume so
bright
Carried by its counting tail it put me out of kilter spoke volumes
where no mass did
I had to stay stock still but it balanced that moment in my mind
and indeed did Consume my absent pal the things left discon-
nected like his people left behind
And made me smile a while it wasn't guile but innate skill that
eased the sting
To and fro it took me in its speed of thought and taught me a de-

licious new Thing In this strange existence we call life! Brain size, what constitutes intelligence, Posed questions of that ilk barb-like caught

I lifted my hat and thought…

The rain melted into vapour as up the track I roamed

pissed off

From that news in that paper now verified

Because I carried ivy for impatient sheep who coughed and bleated

While on this mad caper trailed the creeper

It caught and I looked back in anger

And where the stream is forced down a giant beam after shoots beneath Crookwood lane

It gushes forth boiling froth whence from a half leat

It meets itself and churns white as milk and then widens then to silk still fleet

There dipping alighted near the horizontal crack

Through a funnel beneath the road – it was back

Acting as a pummel loaded pressure pushing water caused rolling waves

Perched above, the soft whisped bobbing bauble

The same bird quite at home and rhythmic its tail a metronome

Grey and yellow in some willow still and low flew down to moss crowned stone

Then up again

It was not frightened of me next that energy

In the sight of human weakness looking back with such reflected meekness and fragility it measured me

On another plane it hopped tipped rolled popped dipped took wing and speared A fly so spry then in the blink of my eye dropped and marked time then plopped amongst clandestine rocky races rills and chases

At such ease in steaming water screes my mind returns there to its world

As soon as it had come it went but in that choreographed swirl of water smoke a moment lasted an eternity and spoke to me

Through that span a gulf of sadness in my human madness it ran

It had cleared my head of heavy thoughts and sent me on my way

A happier man

I Went Out One Night

I went out one night so cold so late
On my return I think
I came back to another place
My soul exploding in a state of effusion
I couldn't close my lid.

Perhaps I was far worse for wear
Then than I imagine now
Some fusion of wine and beer
Had conspired to render me somehow
As the last owl hooted goodbye
I saw a muted star shooting across the milky way
Fade like a firework
Those lights went out the night was dying to a lighter shade
An early cuckoo on its oboe played [blew]

More birds were stirring in translucent trees to sing
Woodquest rehearsed evocative piping notes as if
         invoking strings
With which to mock this false spring
And silent bats were clamouring to roost on tired crinkling wings
The atmosphere was charged with magic things
I let my mind go loose and my wits were maybe dented
For I felt so sure my love was true so confident unrented

Into a revelry I slid I witnessed stars by Orion's Belt
Were switching off their lights too late some secret I may see
Then one shone bright as if it swelled kinetically beyond
         a chanted psalm
And on Orion's belt all hell let loose and on the constellation
shaped Like Swan or goose young cygnets flew away like gold
dust blown From off of an open palm
Brighter than the rest a blue white giantess blew out her breast
Displayed her charm like a princess

Not about to melt to suitors and to answer yes
Betelgeuse on her shoulder so much older
Blood red hot and angry shone – yet another felt her pulse
But with no answer he would not acquiesce

To her he mattered less she would not coalesce
Two great noble giants of different ages
Intransigent in adjacent impasse sat soon ready to go out
And me below heaven bent my arms around my knees spent
Yawned to keep from falling flat
When suddenly raced with a mouse in its face across the lawn a
big black cat…
Both dizzy caused by warping space and pulling moons
Stars tumbled back and in a swoon
Orion consumed the giant the princess and her silver spoon

The great height which I gauged them be sent my mind
        into a roll
My light thoughts took a stroll and entered deep
        inside my soul
Opening up an empty hole
Out of which I felt my true love stole
Escaped and flew beyond the Northern pole
For when I sought out where she lay she'd waited long but hadn't
Stayed again to pour me into bed with her
        – she'd gone away

And so many sad nights since when I return from sodden soirées
I have learned a warning
Not to open up my soul but let it smoulder like a coal let no cold
air rush in
And when in a spin tie my heart up tight if I should stay
To see the night closing on the day
And resist the magic dawning

The Water Vole

Long gone now old ratty from these local waters
The bittern too I never saw and sad they ought to have
Remember the old boys in pubs say as they rubbed
their baccy
How every hay field was smitten by the boom of a bittern
My first cigarette card
Wildlife in Britain
Was of a water vole and an extinct bittern
Hippocampus function in the brain
Sat at the mouth in a shadowy grain
A soft brown memory down a drain
You asked me if I had heard the train
If I'd seen the moon and the sunset wane
And the opening locks
As the water came in with a rush and gush
As down the lane the fishermen homeward bound
Out it came

But all I remember as the memory lasts
The water vole and its repast chewing on a long stem
Til all was gone and starting on another frenetically
Swim like a clockwork chuff chuff train
Back and forth again and again from bank to bank
Sampling herbs and slender reeds
Ignoring birds that stabbed at seed
As it swam swam swam across a lock pound dam
As it seldom heard the wind through willows
Sleeping sound on a bed of mossy pillows
Up with the lark on a river bank to sit on
And remembering as it breakfasted
The long gone bittern

The Song of the Night Sky

I went out one night and hailed to see
Why the silent sky would not shout back at me
Curling galaxies wound silently round
And strangled owls mooted sound
Minstrel suitors serenading
A spinster moon's silver cascadence
Sapped my love I'd held in shadows
And nothing in the glinting gloom
But my mad hours long devoured
By one way love caught in its power

I searched forever in that sky
To hear a cry from the one I'm wishing by
Though could not find the love I trace
Escaping phantom out in space

This sweet melancholic tune
Crescendoed – dived – and rose again
And like a shooting star
Went out of sight
And in clear thoughts which ensued
Shone my true soul
Like a spool unwinding
In a pool of moonlight

Rose in Moonlight

There have been moments
In my past
Where rain and storms and ill
Winds blasted
Paired one to the very core
But now later on in years
Maybe thus more vulnerable
I regret ever I first saw her
For none – like the effect when I discovered
Her true behaviour
Before unbeknown – to me has borne
Such frozen numbing sadness
And compromises cut in half

Long now I had dreamt of one
with joy, gladness
Who like a rose bloomed in the sun.
Whom all the shadows had outshone
Whose love I had supposed I'd won
But unrequited grew and later shunned
Advances that I had begun.
And nervous laughs of apologies
And compromises cut in half

Her breath inhaled twixt kiss on cheeks
Her scent hovered long on my fingertips
On gifts she gave me there it lingered too
I drank it in knowing it was infusing inside
Right through me
Her closeness felt as if connected
Every movement of her eyes dissected
Her slender arms and fingers posed
So delicate yet wholesome woman
Her shyness modesty her simple goodness
So strong

It overbalanced me I laughed
And compromises cut in half

Yet when the winter came along
Autumns fruits fell with silent leaves
And birdsong trailed off
Only echoes of it thread
Through the skeleton wood I walked
A lonely fox coughed
And related to me her empty
Cold and withering song with shivers
Shaking my awkward bones
And petals fell by one by one
A rosehip bud was all that's left
My heart my soul my mind bereft
Concealed her feelings like a nun
So stern not laughing
And compromises cut in half

With residues regret and theft
Her love elsewhere contained such heft
But lived and thrived and grew and bloomed
And no doubt with some other swooned
Entwined in shadows 'neath the moon.
And in that half-light could not see
The merest trace of love for me
But with another cried and laughed
And compromises cut in half.

The Song of a Tramp

I cannot grab that rubber band now broken from your wrist
I've fallen from your hands
A present given with as much love as a golden ring

Slippery the worm it slip slides from my fingertips
While dark grey clouds cause swirlin'
Like dropped skirts overhead
The leaves as they spread
Sped from my boughs
Up and outwards cross the sky now crucified
Are hiding all the thighs that I've opened in the past
And all the lies that that worm is taking with it
As it burrows out of view
Eventually will spew
Down that ever-spinning orifice out in space
That swallows all of our galaxies and hides my shamed face

Sin makes me think
My thoughts flying

Swirling like those skirting clouds round and round
A plug hole in a porcelain sink
Take some time to take it in like drinking in the rain –
Freefalling out of depth
Drenching all your clothes
And then dryin' like some homeless vagrant wretch

A madness always gripping me while basking like a shark
Down by the beaches of the sane
Limping home alone
In a lamplit street of empty houses calling out my name
Even so my stricken mind has closed its eyes on time
I am swimming like a drowning fool
In the reaches of a distant land of dreams!

Lost

No one answered a shout in the distance
Up beyond the Folly wood
But still the call rose and fell
Someone lost some love run off
I could not tell resistance from
Some siren luring me upon the rocks…
Almost like the ringing of an alarm bell
Or in the mist like a buoy near some lost ship
Listing at sea I tumbled in the cloud that descended
I stumbled on not knowing exactly where I was

I could not rest I knew it would come back
I wished to switch it off to cease the agony
The repeated significance of what it said
Or meant
I heard it as it faded away a lament of sorts
As I fumbled my way
Along the frozen fields and down the track
I'd now regained

Upon the lane I kicked my heels
I wanted to escape its haunting echo
When at last it died away
To this day I don't know who or what it was
Nor what the voice was trying to say
As I get on in life the memory is lost in time
But every so often it emerges loud as day
I sometimes think it was only me telling myself
From far off to mind my way

Fall at the Fair

I stood in thought
So the cheers and shouts
The flying people on the merry go round
All went silent not a sound and though it rained
Wet through so deep a hold on me you'd gained

In all that rising falling crowd insane
One chair sped by
Flying empty through the drunken air
I strove to steal a march on my emotions
Held in the prison of my pain

I had run away from that place
Again and again and again
I slipped and fell and down a slope I grappled
For a hold on hope
But down and further down I fell
To a labyrinthine sort of hell

I heard a voice and startled turned
To glimpse across a misty space
A young girl rise rose lipped fine hipped
And freckled face and auburn hair
Beckoning me to follow her

She stooped stopped
I gently pulled and tugged the ties
Which dropped her dress
And bared her soft shoulders
Kissed her neck and held her naked form
So tightly 'til she melted in that misty throng
She gave a glance back which haunts me still
Lasting long and lingering on and on and on – until
Down the corridors of time I see her floating now

It made me double take
And in that second erred
Some doubt within me stirred
Suddenly the thought occurred

She could've been a startled bird I'd caught
Held and stared into its eyes mesmerised
And dreamt the rest
I imagined so absurd I had become

But then I had a thought
So lucid it burned white hot and true
I wondered why we rarely risk and dare
To take the ride right there

In case we do and shout and cry
And fall and die
Expose our true and utmost fears to all who
Walk on by

And never risk in love and choose
A road that's lying there
Which twists and turns and asks so many
Questions of you and I
Is it
Our true heart and inner soul we steer by?

Autumn

A long time now I dream of one
Who like a rose blooms in the sun
Whose love I had supposed I'd won
But unrequited grows
And shuns advances that I had begun

And when the winter comes along
And relates to me her empty cold
And withering song
And petals fall by one by one
A rosehip bud is all that's left
My heart my soul and mind bereft

With feelings of regret and theft
Her love elsewhere contains such heft
But lies and thrives and grows and blooms
And no doubt with this other swoons
Entwined in shadows 'neath the moon

And in that half-light cannot see
The merest trace of love for me
But with another cries and laughs
And compromises cut in half.

The Last Song

Looked up at the gypsy
Labouring under the quilt of clouds
Thinking aloud and gently
Rubbing my finger along
The Turks head

Unflicting pain
A few piano chords strain in the last song
And there you tread out to the fields where
We belong surrounded by buttercups
In the long meadows you come to join me
And how can that be wrong

The mists swirl
The lark rises up
Til she has gone
Nothing is up there with the angels
One messenger falls through the sun's haze
He calls to me
You're the next one

I looked up at the treeline
Through the seed heads
Like a lion would
At the pigeons scatter
Its warm heavy muzzle
Nestled in my lap on
Your soft swan neck
Juices splatter
Like a nightmare

Its eye wrestling nestling settling
Sunk into its prey
As the cuckoo sang in the woods there
All type of things began
All those things we couldn't say

Mark Whelehan

As the day broke and the first bird
Sort of bleated
Like a lamb

Hey don't leave me in this field
Alone naked prone
That chameleon's eye strapped to
The side of my head
Revolving all seeing every single angle
Of the day

Through the binoculars
I watched you all the way
Saw you build your nest
Then try to walk away
Never sleeping seldom seen
Like a nightjar in the day
In the furnace yet the
Hose drips like blood let
By the trough

… And the horse lips tremble shiver
And the horse flies bite 'n buzz
Flanks quiver knee
Deep in Crookwood brook
The whites of its eye turned to look
Startled as you stalk it through
The daisies shrinking
Blinking in the dry scruff…

Do tell me to stop now
I'm getting tired of this play
The nettle stings around my wrist
The moon rising like a cyst
The sun dying like a stye
Inside my eye

The hard steel pulse
The soft buoyant tyres
Kiss the warm tarmac
Settle into the succulent seats
We click the doors shut
Off goes the world
Onto a small screen
Spin the wheel
And purr away

So I looked up at the moth
From the long grass
Hovering as it battled
In the cross-fire
With its wing beats so strong
And so violent
And so silent
Opened the window
And it flies away

I fucked up for so long but
I righted my wrongs
At least I tried to
And that's the main thing

And so it goes on
Til all us are gone
That's the next thing
And the last song

About Mark Whelehan

Mark is a well-known sculptor, and polymath. His early unconventional approach to sculpture – that there are no rules – has seen him described him as a maverick in contemporary practice. Though imagination and original ideas play a huge part in his work, he is not a conceptualist!

He went to Dauntsey's School, Wilt-shire. He has an M.A. in Fine Art from the Arts University College, Bournemouth. He studied art and design at Manchester Metropolitan University and has a B.A. [Hons] in Creative Studies in English from Bath Spa University.

He began his career at the Royal Exchange Theatre, Manchester, where he went from building props for stage productions, into acting. He has held an equity card for 35 years and has subsequently worked in television, theatre and film.

Although he is open-minded he adheres to some conservative principles in sculpture and writing. Provocatively (and para-doxically) he is a progressive modernist, stretching the boundaries. Be it ignoring punctuation to give ambiguity and double explanation, or exploding clay in kiln-firing, or mimic riven rock – whatever it takes to gain a means to justify the ends.

'Beauty is in the eye of the beholder' is an adopted mantra, but the 'idea' is not more important than 'the piece'. He believes good art is originality linked with skill, and that's what he seeks to attain in his work!

He writes creatively and associates his work with poetry and text, sometimes music – often one inspiring the other. He is happiest producing work that combines the aesthetic with the unusual.

His mother Gertrude Swift painted. His Great Uncle Francis Topping was a Benedictine monk and Housemaster at Ampleforth School – an accomplished artist and good friend of the sculptor Henry Moore. Mark's ability maybe came from this side of the family.

Semantics intrigue him… He is a wordsmith influenced by, amongst others, his father Seos Whelehan, Flan O'Brien and James Joyce, and is a fan of The Beatles, Oasis and Shakespeare – in poetry, Wordsworth, Dylan Thomas, W.B. Yates, Robert Frost and W.H. Auden are respected.

Cassiopeia Lying Eastward represents the varied attempts to recreate past and present love, atmosphere, landscapes, folklore and characters from his precious Crookwood (near Devizes, Wiltshire), where he has a couple of acres with a stream running through it!

He says, "My Grandfather used to swim with James Joyce off the Renvyle Peninsular, Galway, Eire. Maybe, hopefully, something in the water accidentally invaded the trunks or genes and filtered down to me!"

Mark teaches sculpture. He keeps it simple, there is no ego involved. He just encourages students to express themselves, and he doesn't expect his students to attempt anything he wouldn't.

"Try the medium and see if it suits!"

His approach is not standing up in front of a class to demonstrate his own skills – unless it's an arranged Master class. He feels that sort of arrogance merely stymies timid people from developing their tentative early ideas.

He doesn't try to fill people's heads with established theories which can deter and exclude many who feel it is beyond them – he reckons there is too much self-esteemed snobbery amongst artists trying to be elitist, who have too high an opinion of themselves and their 'Art': middlemen and sycophants upping their own remunerative antis!

He feels the best approach is subtlety, giving students free reign and inviting and allowing them to call the shots – giving support always guiding if needs be, but direction, advice and help only when asked! His success teaching young and mature students is testament to his open friendly encouraging positive technique and his ability to get his message across to all ages.

website : http://www.markwhelehan.com/

e-mail : markwhelehan01@gmail.com

Ditty Box Publishing

Ditty Box Publishing is located in the Shropshire Hills.

It supports authors, artists, crafters, and entrepreneurs by providing publishing & printing services to the community.

Ditty Box Publishing is a division of Ditty Box Ltd, a company registered in England (No. 4602831).

Contact Details:

Website: dittyboxpublishing.com

E-Mail: admin@dittyboxpublishing.com

Lightning Source UK Ltd.
Milton Keynes UK
UKHW02f1030080118
315737UK00009B/162/P

9 780956 489951